BASIC LIGHTING WORKTEXT FOR FILM AND VIDEO

BASIC LIGHTING WORKTEXT FOR FILM AND VIDEO

RICHARD K. FERNCASE, MFA

Focal Press
Boston   London

iv

Focal Press is an imprint of Butterworth–Heinemann.

 Recognizing the importance of preserving what has been written, it is the policy of Butterworth–Heinemann to have the books it publishes printed on acid-free paper, and we exert our best efforts to that end.

Library of Congress Cataloging-in-Publication Data

Ferncase, Richard K.
   Basic lighting worktext for film and video / by Richard K. Ferncase.
       p.   cm.
   Includes bibliographical references.
   ISBN 0-240-80085-0 (pbk. : alk. paper)
   1. Cinematography—Lighting. 2. Television—Lighting.
I. Title. TR891.F47   1992
778.5′2343—dc20   91–41120
                                                              CIP

British Library Cataloguing in Publication Data

Ferncase, Richard K.
   Basic lighting worktext for film and video.
   I. Title
   778.52343

   ISBN 0–240–80085–0

Butterworth–Heinemann
80 Montvale Avenue
Stoneham, MA 02180

10 9 8 7 6 5 4 3 2 1

Printed in the United States of America

*For my father,
Richard Joseph Ferncase,
1916–1988*

Vademecum—Vadetecum
Es lockt dich mein Art und Sprach,
Du folgest mir, du gehst mir nach?
Geh nur dir selber treulich nach:
So folgest du mir—gemach! gemach!

Friedrich Nietzsche
Die Frohliche Wissenschaft

CONTENTS

PREFACE AND ACKNOWLEDGMENTS

There are several ways to learn a craft—I can think of three, anyway. The first and most effective method is the *mentor-apprentice* method in which the interested student seeks out and works with a master in a given field. This method served the great painters quite well, right up to this century. Unfortunately, there are few masters willing to take assistants under their wings these days.

The second way to learn a craft is the hallowed *learn-by-doing* approach—a favorite of many film schools. Students are shown equipment and are expected to stumble along on their own, making mistakes, spending money, and learning as they go along. This type of learning can lead to a reinvent-the-wheel syndrome, which is not necessarily a bad thing. Learning through one's own experience often provides the most indelible education. The trick is to learn to do things effectively and efficiently (and not go broke in the process).

A third route to learning a craft is by *reading books* devoted to the subject. I admit that this approach by itself is inadequate. The printed page cannot hope to keep abreast of the latest methods, equipment, and trends in a rapidly changing field. But you will find information more readily in books than from any other source available to you.

In this worktext, I have tried to provide a combination of these three methods. Unlike a conventional manual or textbook, this worktext is intended to guide you through a series of practical exercises, self-study quizzes, and projects designed to help reinforce skills learned through applied lighting situations. The self-study questions include multiple choice, true and false, and matching questions that cover much of the material in each chapter. Answers and explanations are given to guide you through this section. The chapter's projects sections provide practical exercises to give guided, hands-on experience. Many of the lighting setups are starting points for situations often encountered in the studio and on location. By using these self-studies, exercises, and projects, I hope that you can *learn by doing*, without wasting too much time and money.

When I started to compile this book, I couldn't find a truly comprehensive and useful, basic text on lighting. Since then, I have found several good books devoted to some aspect of the subject, most of which are included in the bibliography. Some of the books offer detailed information about lighting fixtures and accessories, some present practical lighting procedures used in the field, and some are texts that discuss lighting as an adjunct to cinematography and videography. This book brings together all the information relevant to lighting for film and video production, and presents it in a readable, logical manner. So rather than spending all your time in a research library reading books devoted to the subject, you may, instead, find much of what you need to know right here.

This worktext is designed for those who have some familiarity with filmmaking and videography, and wish to improve their production skills. This book should prove valuable to film and video students, independent filmmakers and videomakers, corporate and industrial production and television professionals, as well as those producers who simply wish to improve the quality of their productions and get an edge on their competition.

This book is organized in three parts. The first part contains four chapters devoted to basic concepts—1) The Visible Spectrum, 2) Film and Exposure, 3) Using Electricity, and 4) Video, the Electronic Medium. The second part covers four important elements of lighting—5) Controlling Color Temperature: Light Sources and Filters, 6) Controlling Light Quality: Lighting Equipment, 7) Measuring Light Intensity, and 8) Manipulating Light: Direction and Balance. The third part of this book is devoted to practical lighting situations—9) Lighting Concepts in Practice, 10) Lighting in the Studio, and 11) Lighting on Location. In these final chapters, I have attempted to cover many of the fine points of lighting style by drawing from the great cinematographers regarding diverse lighting topics from motivation to the psychology of color. Thus, you may also benefit, albeit indirectly, from the wisdom and experience of accomplished professionals—your *mentors*.

Many of the projects in this book use photographic film as part of the project. If you wish, however, you may use video for all the projects (except the Chapter 2 film project), if you have access to a video camcorder or camera and VCR.

The term *cinematographer* is used throughout this book to refer to the person in charge of production lighting design; its use is not intended to slight the video or television producer. Depending on the type of production, *cinematographer* may refer to the lighting director, the director of photography, the videographer, the photographer, or the filmmaker. Similarly, I often refer to a production as a *film*, because I prefer this term to its less exact alternatives—video, show, or program.

I am indebted to many people for their help and encouragement, especially my colleagues at Chapman University, including Ron Thronson, Jay Boylan, Richard Doetkett, and Gregory Hobson. Thanks to my first film professor, Brian Lewis, who encouraged me in my early days as a filmmaker. Thanks to Dana Blumer who proofread early versions of the manuscript. Thanks also to Rosco Laboratories, Inc., and Lowel Lighting for their assistance. I am especially grateful to Karen Speerstra, Sharon Falter, and the rest of the editorial staff at Focal Press for their encouragement and help. Without their assistance, this tome would have never seen the, well, light of day.

BASIC LIGHTING WORKTEXT FOR FILM AND VIDEO

CHAPTER ONE

The Visible Spectrum

INTRODUCTION

What we know about light goes back long before film and video were invented, and is the result of the findings of several scientists and engineers. Over the course of time, two fundamental, opposing theories of light gradually evolved and competed for dominance in the field of optical science for centuries before they were integrated into one theory by Einstein and others in the twentieth century.

Sir Isaac Newton described light as being composed of tiny particles (or corpuscles) of radiant matter. Newton's corpuscle theory, however, accepted largely on the basis of his other outstanding achievements in physics and mathematics, could not explain several properties of light, such as diffraction.

By the beginning of the eighteenth century, Newton's contemporary, Christian Huygens, had popularized the wave theory of light. According to Huygens' principle, light traveled as vibrational disturbances, similar to sound waves, through the "ether" of space. Huygens' wave theory gradually took precedence over Newton's corpuscle theory.

In the late nineteenth century, James Clerk Maxwell enunciated his electromagnetic theory and described light as a vibration of electric and magnetic waves. Maxwell went on to explain that visible light is but a small portion of a wide-ranging spectrum of electric and magnetic waveforms, with frequencies that vary in length.

Maxwell's theory was proven in 1887 by Heinrich Hertz, who demonstrated the existence of electromagnetic waveforms by transmitting and receiving them in his laboratory. His experiments led to the development of wireless telegraphy, radio, and television.

In 1905, Albert Einstein suggested a return to a modified version of Newton's theory when he published his concept of photons, or subatomic radiant particles, with the premise that "energy clumps" travel in straight lines, which our eyes perceive as light. Thus, light is now considered a duality that consists of both particles and waves.

THE ELECTROMAGNETIC SPECTRUM

Light travels in straight lines at a constant speed of 186,282 miles per second (mps) and moves in all directions as a transverse wave (see Figure 1.1). Light comprises a very small part of the continuum known as the *electromagnetic spectrum*, which also includes gamma rays and X rays, radio waves, and alternating electrical current (see Figure 1.2). The

FIGURE 1.1 Light as a transverse wave. Light waves vibrate in all planes perpendicular to the direction of propagation.

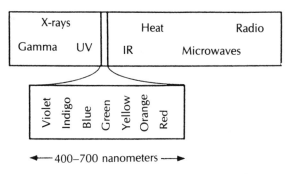

← 400–700 nanometers →

FIGURE 1.2 Visible light comprises a very small portion of the radiant energy in the electromagnetic spectrum.

radiant energy of the spectrum is classified according to *wavelength*—the distance between successive waves.

The shortest wavelengths, the cosmic rays, are so small that there are billions of waves to the inch. The longest waves, electrical power waves, measure several miles in length. Physicists use the metric nanometer, or millimicron (one-thousandth of a millimeter), as the measurement of light wavelength. Energies of very long wavelength, such as radio waves, are generally measured by frequency of wave cycles per second, or *Hertz*. As the speed of electromagnetic energy is constant, frequency is inversely proportional to the wavelength. In other words, the shorter the wavelength, the higher its frequency; the longer the wavelength, the lower its frequency. The wavelength of visible light is discernible to the eye as *hue*.

1

WHITE LIGHT

White light, with wavelengths that measure 400–700 nanometers, is actually the sum of hues in the visible spectrum. The hues of the spectrum may be observed in a rainbow or when white light passes through a prism. Newton, who had a predilection for the mystic number seven, identified the spectral primary hues as violet, indigo, blue, green, yellow, orange, and red. The "cool" hues (violet, indigo, blue, and green) have short wavelengths, while the "warm" hues (yellow, orange, and red) have longer wavelengths. Invisible light that has a shorter wavelength than violet is known as *ultraviolet*; light with wavelengths longer than red, which includes heat, is called *infrared*. Although the human eye cannot see ultraviolet and infrared radiation, photographic and video media are sensitive to these wavelengths. Film, in particular, is sensitive to heat, which occurs primarily in the infrared band of the spectrum.

The seven colors of the rainbow notwithstanding, for photographic and technical purposes, it is now standard practice to consider white light in terms of its three *additive primary colors*—red, green, and blue (see Figure 1.3). The secondary or *subtractive primary colors* are magenta (red and blue), cyan (green and blue), and yellow (green and red).

SPECULAR AND DIFFUSED LIGHT

Light that emanates from a pointlike source and strikes a subject from a single angle or from a few, very similar angles is said to have a *specular* quality. Specular light is hard, sharp, well-directed, and casts distinct, dense shadows. A prime specular light source is the sun.

When light strikes a subject from a variety of different angles as a result of scattering by an intermediate medium, it is called *diffused light*. Diffused light tends to be soft, even, and flat; its shadows are less dense and less defined (see Figure 1.4). When clouds cover the sun, the resulting illumination is diffused.

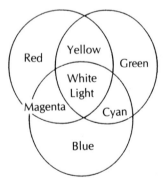

FIGURE 1.3 White light divided into its additive and subtractive primaries—red, green, blue, magenta, cyan, and yellow.

PROPERTIES OF LIGHT

When light strikes the surface of another medium, it may be

reflected—bounced back into the original medium
absorbed—converted by the new medium into another form of energy, such as heat
transmitted and/or refracted—propagated through the new medium at an angle determined by the angle of incidence (direction of falling light) and the relative densities of the two media

Reflection

Reflection, like direct illumination, may be specular or diffused. Specular reflection occurs when specular light strikes a shiny surface, such as a mirror or aluminum foil. In this case, specular light always bounces off the surface at an angle equal to the angle of incidence (see Figure 1.5). In other words, the angle of incidence is equal to the angle of reflectance.

Diffused reflection is the result of light striking an irregular or matte (dull) surface. Rays that strike this type of surface will be split up and reflected in many different directions (see Figure 1.6).

Mixed reflection, a combination of diffused and specular reflection, results when light strikes a wet, oily, glossy, or polished surface. In such instances, light is reflected in a

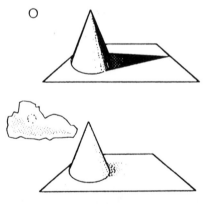

FIGURE 1.4 Specular light, which emanates from an apparent small source such as the sun, produces distinct, dense shadows. Diffused light emanates from a large source, such as the open sky or clouds that cover the sun.

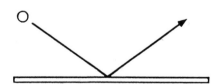

FIGURE 1.5 Specular reflection.

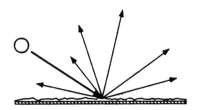

FIGURE 1.6 Diffused reflection.

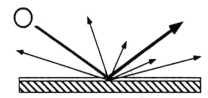

FIGURE 1.7 Mixed or partial reflection.

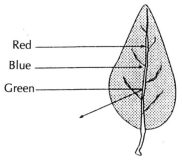

Red
Blue
Green

FIGURE 1.8 Absorption.

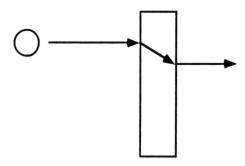

FIGURE 1.9 Refraction.

FIGURE 1.10 Refraction—the apparent bending of a spoon in a glass of water.

specular fashion from the shiny top layer and diffused from the surface (see Figure 1.7).

Absorption

Light that is neither reflected nor transmitted is said to be *absorbed*. The color of a surface is determined by those wavelengths that are reflected and those that are absorbed by the surface. A green object absorbs light of shorter wavelengths, mostly blue and red hues, and reflects light of longer wavelengths, thus producing a green hue (see Figure 1.8). Objects that absorb light equally from all parts of the spectrum appear white, black, or gray.

Transmission

As light strikes a transparent medium (clear glass, for example), some of the light is reflected, a little is absorbed, but most of it passes through or is *transmitted* by the medium. A colored medium transmits its own color and absorbs all others.

A translucent material (like waxed paper) permits some light to pass, but, due to surface texture or composition, scatters light and prevents clear visibility through the medium. No light passes through an opaque medium. The amount of light reflected depends on surface absorption, color, texture, and the angle of incidence.

Refraction

Although light travels through space at a constant 186,282 mps, its speed is only three-fourths as great in clear liquids and two-thirds as great in transparent solids. When light passes from one medium to another of greater density, it slows and changes direction; the light is *refracted*. Refraction is the bending of light as it slows when it passes from one transparent medium, such as air, to another of a different density, such as water (see Figure 1.9). Refraction can be observed as the apparent bending of a spoon in a clear glass of water (see Figure 1.10).

Self-Study

■ QUESTIONS

1. Light travels as _____.
   a. waves
   b. particles
   c. waves and particles
2. The nanometer is a measurement of light _____.
   a. frequency
   b. quality
   c. wavelength
3. Visible light comprises a small part of the electromagnetic spectrum at wavelenghts measuring between _____.
   a. 2900–10,000° Kelvin
   b. 820–2500 kiloHertz
   c. 400–700 nanometers
4. White light is made up of the primary colors red, blue, and _____.
   a. cyan
   b. yellow
   c. green
5. Light that strikes a subject from a number of angles is said to have a _____ quality.
   a. diffused
   b. specular
   c reflected
6. Heat occurs primarily in the _____ band of the electromagnetic spectrum.
   a. infrared
   b. ultraviolet
   c. X-ray
7. The property of light that causes it to bend when passing through translucent solids or liquids is called _____.
   a. diffraction
   b. absorption
   c. refraction
8. Energies of long wavelength, such as radio waves, are measured by _____.
   a. frequency
   b. wavelength
   c. electrical charge
9. When light is absorbed by a surface, it _____.
   a. disappears
   b. is transformed into heat
   c. is reflected
10. Photographic film is sensitive to heat, a form of _____ light.
    a. infrared
    b. ultraviolet
    c. X-ray

■ ANSWERS

1. **c.** While a. and b. are both partly right, c. is the most appropriate answer, as light is now recognized as a wave and particle form of energy.
2. **c.** The nanometer, one billionth of a meter, is the standard measurement of light wavelength. Longer wavelengths of energy, such as microwaves and radio waves, are measured according to frequency (or how many times they occur per second) in Hertz; thus they are known as *Hertzian waves*.

3. **c.** The spectrum of visible light ranges in wavelength from 400–700 nanometers. Kelvin is a measure of light color temperature and is discussed in Chapter Five. KiloHertz refers to frequencies of the electromagnetic spectrum that include AM radio waves.

4. **c.** White light is the sum total of the additive primaries red, blue, and green. Cyan and yellow, along with magenta, are the subtractive hues. Cyan is a combination of blue and green, yellow is made up of green and red, and magenta is an equal mixture of red and blue.

5. **a.** Light that strikes a subject from various angles is considered diffused. Specular light emanates from a pointlike source and thus strikes a subject at a single angle or very few angles.

6. **a.** Heat occurs almost exclusively in the longer wavelengths of invisible light known as *infrared*. Ultraviolet radiation, which includes light of shorter wavelengths, is emitted profusely from the sky as well as the tubes in tanning booths; it is not inherently hot. X rays are even shorter in length and also do not register as heat.

7. **c.** When light passes from one translucent medium to another of a different density, such as from air to water, it changes direction and appears to bend; this is called *refraction*. Diffraction, a phenomenon of all waveform energy, occurs as light rays pass near the edges of an opening or through a small hole, resulting in prismatic color break up due to interference (diffraction can be observed as a rainbow effect on the fringe of the pool of light cast by certain lensed fixtures). Absorption occurs when visible light is transformed to another energy form, such as heat.

8. **a.** It is more convenient to measure long-wave radiation, such as radio waves, according to the frequency of the waveform (measured in cycles per second or Hertz), rather than by wavelength, which can span miles. Electrical charge has no bearing on wavelength or frequency in this case.

9. **b.** See answer to #7 for explanation.

10. **a.** Photographic film is sensitive to much of the radiant energy of the electromagnetic spectrum, including X rays, ultraviolet light, and infrared radiation. Heat is found, however, only in the infrared portion of the spectrum.

■ PROJECT 1.1: SPLITTING WHITE LIGHT INTO ITS COMPONENT HUES

Purpose:

To demonstrate the visible spectrum.

Materials Needed:

a triangular prism (available from Edmund Scientific Co.; 101 E. Gloucester Pike; Barrington, NJ; USA; 08007–1380 or any hobby supply company)
an 8½ × 11-inch sheet of white paper
the sun or other specular source

Procedure:

1. Many of Sir Isaac Newton's experiments with visible light centered around his use of the prism and you can duplicate his demonstrations as well. Hold the prism in a beam of sunlight, so that the sun or other hard light strikes the prism.
2. Turn the prism until it casts a rainbow on the white paper.
3. Note the arrangement of hues in the spectrum. Newton noted seven colors in the rainbow. How many colors can you discern and identify? What physical property of light causes white light to split into separate hues? How does the shape of the prism bring this about?

■ PROJECT 1.2: PROPERTIES OF VISIBLE LIGHT

Purpose:

To demonstrate various properties of light.

Materials Needed:

8 × 10-inch (or similar size) mirror
8 × 10-inch (or similar size) pane of clear glass
8 × 10-inch gray card (18% reflectance) (available at any camera store)
8 × 10-inch matte black card (a black notebook cover will do)
flashlight or penlight
clear glass of water
spoon
a room that can be darkened

Procedure:

1. Lay the mirror, shiny side up, on a table or desk top. Point the lighted flashlight at a wall and note the appearance of the beam. Then angle the light toward the mirror at a 45° angle. Change the angle and note how the angle of reflection changes to match the angle of incidence. This is specular reflection.
2. Repeat the last step using the white side of the gray card. Turn the card over so that the gray side is face up. Notice how the light reflects in a scattered fashion. Light reflects over a wide area on a white surface and in a much more subdued fashion (diffused light) on the gray side of the card.
3. Lay the sheet of glass over the gray card and shine the light again. Notice that the light now reflects in a specular fashion off the shiny surface of the glass *and* as diffused light from the underlying matte surface of the card. This is mixed reflection.
4. Repeat this step a final time using the black surface instead of the card and glass. See that there is very little reflection, as most of the light is absorbed.
5. Take the spoon and place it in the water. Notice how the spoon appears to separate as it passes beneath the surface of the water. This is an example of refraction.

Film and Exposure

INTRODUCTION

Any discussion of lighting must consider the medium that collects the light. All cameras imitate the human eye, incorporating the light-gathering lens and the regulating iris. The eye forms its image on the light-sensitive retina, which is analogous to photographic film and the video target.

HOW FILM WORKS

Film consists of a clear plastic base (usually cellulose triacetate or polyester) coated on one side with a photographic emulsion. The emulsion is made up of light-sensitive silver halide crystals suspended in a thin layer of gelatin. A top coat protects the emulsion from scratches (see Figure 2.1). In reversal films, a black antihalation backing is added to eliminate halo effects in the bright highlights and prevent light from penetrating the film base and reflecting off shiny metallic parts inside the camera back.

Color films, using a subtractive color process, have three emulsion layers, each of which is sensitive to cyan, magenta, and yellow, respectively. Each layer filters, or subtracts, a portion of the white light passing through the film. During film processing, the silver halide crystals are replaced with corresponding dyes to create the color image. The film is exposed to a controlled amount of light through a lens. Objects within the lens' field of view reflect varying and distinct amounts of light, creating a latent image of the scene on the photochemically sensitive silver halide crystals in the emulsion. The film is later developed and the crystals are fixed in the processing lab, creating a *negative* (or *reversed tonality image*) of the photographed scene.

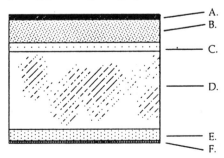

FIGURE 2.1 Cross section of panchromatic film showing protective coating (A), light-sensitive emulsion (B), first adhesive layer (C), plastic base (D), second adhesive layer (E), and antihalation coating (F).

NEGATIVE AND REVERSAL FILMS

Most people who have used a camera are familiar with negative film, which requires printing to produce a positive picture. Reversal film undergoes an extra step during processing to reverse the negative image to create an original positive. Reversal films include transparency and slide films, which may be viewed without having to be printed. Color photography for illustration and print work is often done in reversal. In the past, much 16mm filmmaking was done in reversal, because it was cheaper and cleaner than working with negative film. Now, however, improved negative materials and laboratory procedures have made reversal filmmaking a thing of the past.

Reversal films tend to be higher in contrast than negative emulsions and produce rich, saturated colors. Because reversal films are designed for projection and direct viewing, they have too much inherent contrast to print well. They also have inherently less latitude (i.e., margin for error) during exposure than negative stocks, thus making proper exposure critical. Black-and-white reversal stocks also tend to be slightly less light-sensitive than their negative counterparts.

SENSITOMETRY

The science of measuring a film's sensitivity to light is called *sensitometry*. A practical understanding of sensitometry does not require a degree in math or physics, but does require some common sense.

A popular misconception is that any given scene requires but one "correct" exposure—a notion perpetuated by the widespread adoption of automatic exposure cameras. Instead, proper exposure always depends on the effect desired by the photographer.

Every scene contains a number of reflected *brightnesses*, or values. Film is capable of reproducing only a fraction of the values seen by the human eye. An outdoor scene may include a range of values from a brilliant white sky to a black pole in deep shadow. The eye accommodates these tonal extremes by darting imperceptibly among them and simultaneously compensating for their differences. The camera lens takes in the entire scene, but the film cannot accurately record extremes of value occurring within that scene, as its range is much more limited. Therefore, it is up to the photographer to decide which elements in a scene are important and to calculate an exposure that will include those elements within the range that the film will faithfully reproduce.

EXPOSURE INDEX

For practical purposes, the sensitivity of every film is rated by its *exposure index* (EI). The higher the EI, the faster and more light-sensitive the film. Traditionally, in the United States, EI has been commonly referred to by American Standards Association (ASA) numbers. However, the ASA number has been phased out by Kodak and other manufacturers in favor of those numbers decreed by the International Standards Organization (ISO), which includes the European Deutsch Industrie Norm index (DIN). ASA and ISO refer to the same system, but nowadays exposure indices are labeled on nearly all film packages as ISO numbers. A film's EI is often stated as part of the trade name (e.g., AGFA XT-*320*.

The EI increases by a factor of two as the light sensitivity of the film doubles. Therefore, a film with an EI of 200 is twice as light-sensitive (or fast) as an EI 100 film. EI is also directly related to a lens' f-stop and camera shutter speed. A film of EI 50 requires one f-stop more of light than an EI 100 film under similar conditions. *As the EI doubles, the film is rated twice as sensitive and requires half as much light for exposure.*

The relationship between film speeds are often described as differences in *stops*. A stop represents an increase of a factor of two or a decrease by one half. Thus, Ektachrome 200 film may be considered three stops faster than Kodachrome 25, because 25 doubled three times equals 200. This concept is important to grasp, as it is commonly used in professional photography and filmmaking.

THE CHARACTERISTIC CURVE

The range of a film may be charted on a graph as a characteristic curve. The curve represents the relationship between light levels and densities for a given emulsion. Consider an interior scene that includes a seated figure in front of a sunny window (see Figure 2.2). Shadows tend to become crushed together at the toe end of the film's characteristic curve, while details in full sun are mostly lost, blocking up at the shoulder of the curve. The extreme values of light and dark are beyond the resolving abilities of the film—they fall outside of its characteristic curve (see Figure 2.3).

The ideal film range is represented as a continuous, straight, 45° line. Unfortunately, no such film exists. The closest thing to an ideal film is the straight portion of the curve. Any inherently low-contrast scene is within the limits of the straight portion of the curve and is faithfully reproduced in correctly related values. The shape of the characteristic curve provides specific information about film speed, latitude, and contrast.

Film Speed

Film speed refers to the sensitivity of the emulsion to light and is expressed by the position of the characteristic curve in

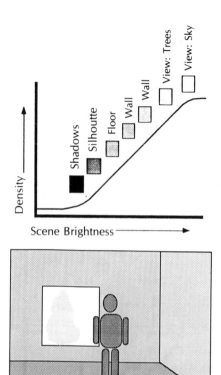

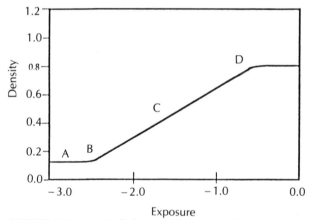

FIGURE 2.2 Contrast range of a room interior.

FIGURE 2.3 A typical characteristic curve illustrates how a film's density increases with exposure. The inherent density of the film base, including some fogging (inherent translucence of the film base, which diffuses blacks to some degree), is represented at (A). Details of a scene dark enough to fall in this portion are not reproduced. (B) is where small amounts of light begin to become exposed. The straight portion (C) of the curve shows how density increases proportionately with exposure. (D) marks the point where increased exposure no longer produces any significant density change; highlights are blocked up and lose detail beyond this point.

relation to the horizontal scale (scene brightness). Fast films are more sensitive than slow films; this makes them better suited for low-light shooting. As a fast film responds to light more rapidly, its characteristic curve slopes upward on the graph before that of a slower film (see Figure 2.4).

Latitude

Latitude refers to a film's degree of tolerance for error in exposure (i.e., how much the exposure can be off and still produce a good picture) and the range of tones that a film is capable of reproducing. Latitude may be measured on the characteristic curve as the difference between the scene brightness range and the film's exposure range (represented as the straight portion of the curve from the toe to the shoulder). A few rules to remember about exposure are as follows:

The wider the scene brightness range, the higher the contrast of the scene.
The steeper the characteristic curve, the higher the contrast of the film.
Latitude decreases as contrast increases.

PUSHING FILM

Many films can be *force processed* or *pushed* one or two stops to double or quadruple their effective speed. This procedure involves increasing a film's development time to bring out more of the image. Indeed, there are some films like Ektachrome 800/1600 designed especially for this purpose. To push a film, simply treat it as a double (or four times) its normal EI rating and tell the film processing lab to put it one stop (or two). Thus, an EI 50 film may be exposed as an EI 200 film. This is useful when shooting under low light conditions. However, pushing film also creates a grainier, more contrasty image, as it steepens the characteristic curve of the film. Thus, the greater the film development time, the higher the contrast.

FLASHING FILM

Sometimes a film is *post-fogged* or *flashed* in order to reduce its inherent contrast. Flashing involves re-exposing the film to a weak light source before processing, in order to fog it slightly. A projection contrast film, such as Eastman Kodak's video news film, is sometimes flashed when prints are required. Post-fogged scenes usually have soft desaturated colors and shimmering, gossamerlike highlights.

RECIPROCITY

Exposure is governed by an interdependent relationship between light intensity (f-stop) and time (shutter speed):

$$exposure = intensity \times time$$

If either the intensity of light or its period of duration are halved, the other variable must be doubled in order to arrive at the same exposure. For example, a shutter speed of $1/60$ with an aperture of 8 produces the same exposures as $1/125$ at f/5.6. A shift from a shutter speed of $1/60$ to $1/125$ results in 50% less light reaching the film. For consistent exposure, one must reciprocate by increasing the aperture size by one stop from f/8 to f/5.6, which doubles the light intensity. This *law of reciprocity*, as it is known, is constant for all but very long (more than 1 second) or very short (less than .001 second) exposure times.

Filmmakers generally have fewer options than photographers in terms of reciprocity, because they must shoot at a constant frame rate (24 frames per second) for normal, synchronous, sound filming. This translates to a fixed shutter speed of anywhere from $1/48-1/64$ second. Because of this, lighting for motion pictures is generally more complex than lighting for still photography.

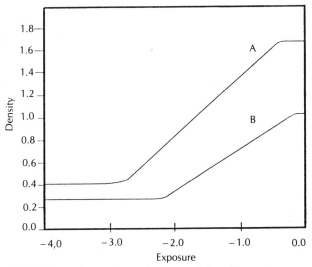

FIGURE 2.4 Comparison of a fast and slow film. The curve of the fast film (A) begins to slope before the curve of the less sensitive film (B). Curve A also shows more inherent fog (depicted as the higher toe portion) in the fast film, which is seen at the base of the curve and the relative steepness of the straight portion of the curve, as compared to B.

FILM STORAGE

Film is sensitive to humidity and electromagnetic radiation beyond the visible light spectrum, including infrared, ultraviolet, X-ray, and cosmic radiation. Fogging and color contrast shifts will result if the emulsion is exposed to any of these wavelengths.

High humidity causes film to become sticky and encourages the growth of mold. Raw stock (unexposed film), therefore, should be stored in an area of 70% or less relative humidity. Processed film should be kept at a relative humidity between 40% and 50%.

Heat, which includes infrared light, will fog film and alter its color rendition. Therefore, it is advisable to store raw stock in its original can at a temperature of 55° Fahrenheit (F) (13° Celsius (C)) for no longer than 6 months. For long-term storage, a temperature of −10° to 0°F (−23° to −18°C) is recommended. After removing a package of raw stock from cold storage, allow it to warm to room temperature before unsealing the can. This will prevent telescoping, or loosening, of the roll during handling as well as film spotting due to moisture condensation. Exposed film should be processed as soon as possible. In the meantime, it should be stored at a temperature of no more than 70°F (21°C).

X rays may fog film, particularly high-speed emulsions. Always try to personally carry film and have it checked by hand when traveling through airline X-ray checkpoints. In some cases, this may not be possible, due to ever-tightening security in international airports. Therefore, be aware that X-ray fogging is a cumulative phenomenon and each pass through radiation will increase an emulsion's fog level. One or two passes through X-ray radiation may not have a noticeable effect on the film, but five or six passes may. Certain overseas terminals, notably Hong Kong and Frankfurt, Germany, inflict much higher radiation doses during baggage checks than do domestic airports. Furthermore, some airport personnel will not allow hand searches. In these cases, film may be stored in commercially available, lead-lined bags, which will deflect some of the harmful rays.

Despite measures taken to protect film from visible light, heat, and X rays, nothing will protect film from the barrage of ultra-shortwave cosmic radiation, which constantly bombards the earth from outer space. Film is a perishable and as it ages it will exhibit increases in fogging, contrast, and color shifts. Therefore, it is wise to use film before its expiration date.

Self-Study

■ QUESTIONS

1. The steeper a film's characteristic curve, the higher the _____ of the film.
   a. latitude
   b. contrast
   c. resolution
2. The retina of the eye acts like the _____ of a camera.
   a. lens
   b. film
   c. iris
3. Reversal film produces a direct _____ image.
   a. positive
   b. negative
   c. halftone
4. A numerically high exposure index indicates a _____ film.
   a. fast
   b. slow
   c. color
5. All things being equal, an ISO 100 film stock requires _____ stops more exposure than an ISO 400 stock.
   a. one
   b. two
   c. four
6. A film's degree of tolerance for exposure error is known as _____.
   a. reciprocity
   b. luminous intensity
   c. latitude
7. A laboratory procedure for decreasing inherent contrast in a film is called _____
   a. forced processing

    b. post-flashing
    c. bleaching
8. Reciprocity states that exposure = intensity × time. Intensity may be controlled by adjusting the _____.
    a. aperture
    b. shutter speed
    c. frame-per-second (fps) rate
9. With negative film, any portion of a scene that falls beyond the shoulder of the characteristic curve will print as

    _____.
    a. black
    b. gray
    c. white
10. Film is sometimes pushed to increase its speed. Pushing also increases _____.
    a. resolution
    b. contrast
    c. quality

■ ANSWERS

1. b. The characteristic curve of a film is the curve plotted on a graph that illustrates the change of density that occurs in an image as exposure is increased. The steeper the curve, the less the area of tonal variations (gray scale) between black and white—this means a higher contrast film. High-contrast film has relatively little latitude that allows for an image of satisfactory density.

2. b. The retina is the light-sensitive element of the eye and is analogous to photographic film (or the video target). The lens and iris perform the same functions in both the eye and the camera—the lens collects and focuses an image, while the iris controls the amount of light passing through the lens.

3. a. All film registers a latent image in reversed or negative tones. Reversal film undergoes an extra step that reverses the image and produces a direct, positive image without printing a negative. A halftone is a graphic arts process that turns continuous tones of photographs into black-and-white dots for reproduction.

4. a. The EI is the number given a film stock by a manufacturer to indicate its sensitivity. The higher the EI, the faster the film. The EI has no bearing on whether a film is black-and-white or color.

5. b. ISO 400 film is four times faster than ISO 100 stock; a stop is an increase of a factor of two or a decrease of one half. Therefore, an ISO 400 film is 2 stops faster than an ISO 100 film.

6. c. The correct answer is latitude—the range of exposure film will allow and still produce a satisfactory exposure. Reciprocity states that film exposure is dependent on both light intensity and duration. Luminous intensity is the light emitted from a light source (explained in detail in Chapter Six).

7. b. Post-flashing, a controlled method of fogging after exposure, is often used to desaturate hues and add diffusion to a film, thus reducing its inherent contrast. Forced processing, which ostensibly increases a film's speed, increases contrast as well as boosts base fog, the overall fog level that increases when film is developed for longer periods. This fog prevents reproduction of a true black. Bleaching, sometimes done to decrease density in panchromatic films, is a regular step in color film processing when color dyes take the place of silver halides.

8. a. Light intensity is controlled by augmenting or subtracting light before it reaches the film. This is done by changing the size of the lens aperture. The other factor that determines exposure, which is time, is controlled by adjusting the duration of the camera's shutter speed. Shutter speed in motion picture cameras is dependent on the fps rate (24 fps for synchronous sound dialogue speed). Cinema fps and ss must remain consistent with projection conventions.

9. c. The shoulder of the characteristic curve indicates the point beyond which all values are reproduced as white, despite whatever subtle tonalities and detail exist in the scene. Various shades of grays (continuous tonalities) are reproduced in the straight portion of the curve, while the toe represents the area where all tones are rendered as black. The density of black depends on the level of base fog that exists in a film.

10. b. Forced processing or pushing film decreases apparent resolution by developing more silver halides into metallic silver, which increases graininess and softens the image. Hence, quality suffers. The longer development time steepens the film's characteristic curve and results in fewer discernable shades of gray and increased contrast.

■ PROJECT 2.1: USING FAST AND SLOW FILMS

Purpose:

To compare characteristics of various speed films.

Materials Needed:

one roll of 24-exposure Kodak Ektachrome 100 or equivalent
one roll of 24-exposure Kodak Extrachrome 800/1600 or equivalent
camera and tripod
camera log (see Figure 2.5) and pencil

You will shoot the same subjects with both films—one is a medium-speed and one is a high-speed film designed for forced processing. (Rate the high-speed film at ISO 1600.) Go through the following steps with one film loaded in the camera, then reload the camera with the second film and repeat the steps. Be sure to record the following data in your camera log for both films:

exposure number
f-stop
shutter speed
lighting conditions
subject

Procedure:

1. Choose a dense, contrasty landscape image with visible trees, grass, sky, etc. With the sun behind you, shoot the same shot three times with the shutter speed constant and

   at the aperture setting which the camera's light meter indicates is correct
   with the aperture one stop larger
   with the aperture one stop smaller

3. Find a flat, unmodulated area, such as a smooth wall or the open sky, and include no other elements in the frame. Shoot three exposures with the shutter speed constant and

   at the aperture setting which the camera's light meter indicates is correct
   with the aperture one stop larger
   with the aperture one stop smaller

3. Compose this shot in a dimly lit interior, such as a darkly furnished room. Do not use any supplementary lighting, but include a window to the outside somewhere in the composition. Shoot three exposures with the shutter speed constant and

   at the aperture setting which the camera's light meter indicates is correct
   with the aperture one stop larger
   with the aperture two stops larger
   with the aperture one stop smaller
   with the aperture two stops smaller

4. With the remaining exposures, shoot a variety of high-contrast and low-contrast subjects. Remember to include photographs of the same subjects on both rolls of film.
5. Have the rolls processed at a professional color film processing lab. Have the ISO 100 film processed normally, but force process the ISO 1600 film.
6. Review and compare both sets of processed slides. Which film appears to be more grainy? Which film

has the greater exposure latitude? How would the characteristic curve of each film compare to one another? How would the choice of film influence and be influenced by the lighting strategy for any given scene?

CAMERA LOG	PROJECT				FILM TYPE:	
EXPOSURE.	GROUP #	F/STOP	SH. SPD.	FILTER USED	LIGHT RATIO	SHOT DESCRIPTION

FIGURE 2.5 Camera log.

CHAPTER THREE

Using Electricity

INTRODUCTION

The earliest films were photographed by the light of the sun. Professional motion picture and video production have since come to rely heavily on electrical power to operate cameras, sound equipment, and lighting instruments. Since electricity is essential for all artificial lighting, it is necessary to understand its properties, uses, and potential hazards before handling lighting equipment.

ELEMENTS OF ELECTRICITY

All matter is composed of minute units called *atoms*. Each atom consists of a nucleus, which is made up of protons and neutrons, and a number of orbiting particles called *electrons*. An electron carries a negative electrical charge, a proton is positively charged, and a neutron has a neutral charge. Not all electrons are attached to atoms; electrons that move independently from an atom are called *free electrons*. Free electrons that move in the same direction create an electrical current.

A medium in which free electrons move easily is called a *conductor*. Metals, which have many free electrons, are the best conductors. Materials like plastic and rubber, which have few free electrons, actually block the flow of electrical current (see Figure 3.1) and are called *insulators*. Copper wire is a good conductor of electricity; the plastic that encases the wire is a good insulator. An electrical current that flows in a complete, conducting path (including its power source) is called a *circuit*.

ELECTRICAL UNITS

Electricity flowing through a wire can be compared to water running through a hose. Pressure forces water into the hose at the faucet; the higher the pressure, the more water passes through the faucet. Similarly, pressure forces electrons through a wire; this phenomenon is known as *electromotive force*. This force, or *electrical potential*, is measured in *volts*. The greater the pressure, the higher the voltage.

The amount of water flowing through the hose may be measured by how much water comes out of the nozzle in one second. The amount of electrical current that flows past a given point in one second is measured in the same way. The unit of measure of electrical current is called the *ampere* or, more simply, *amp*.

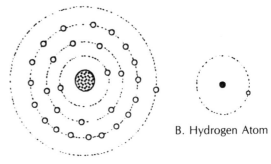

B. Hydrogen Atom

A. Copper Atom

FIGURE 3.1 Atoms of highly conductive metals, such as copper (A), have a single electron that orbits in the outermost valence that facilitates the flow of free electrons. Insulators, such as plastic and rubber, are composed of polymers of hydrogen (B) and carbon, which have simpler, relatively more stable atoms that act to block the flow of electricity.

It is easier to force water through a hose than it is to force water through a drinking straw. The smaller diameter of the straw tends to impede the flow of water. Similarly, a small-diameter wire resists electrical flow more than a large-diameter cable. This resistance is measured in *ohms*.

The ability of electrical energy to do work in a specific time is called *electrical power*. The amount of power in a circuit in which a current of 1 ampere moves across a potential of 1 volt is equal to 1 watt.

Therefore, electricity may be measured by

potential or *electromotive force*, which is measured in *volts*
current, which is measured in *amperes*
power, which is measured in *watts*
resistance, which is measured in *ohms*

For any circuit, the electrical current is directly proportional to the voltage and is inversely proportional to the resistance. Also, power is equal to voltage multiplied by amperage.

DIRECT CURRENT

There are two ways that electricity may flow through a circuit—as *direct current* or *alternating current*. Direct current (DC) flows through a circuit in one continuous direction, while alternating current (AC) intermittently reverses its directional flow (see Figure 3.2).

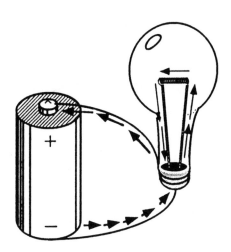

FIGURE 3.2 Electrical current always flows from negative to positive in a circuit. Direct current as shown in this illustration always flows in one direction, as with dry cells and battery power sources. Alternating current, used to transmit electricity over long distances, changes direction 120 times per second (60 Hz).

Batteries and generators are the most common sources of direct current. *Wet cell batteries* produce electricity through a chemical reaction between an acid and a metal. A good example of a wet cell battery can be found under the hood of an automobile. The prime advantage of the wet cell is its rechargeability. Unfortunately, the voltage produced is low. A typical storage battery generates 12 volts, but most lighting fixtures require 110–120 volts. Thus, it takes ten 12-volt batteries to provide enough voltage to light a standard lamp at 3200° Kelvin (K). Wet cell batteries are also usually heavy and cumbersome.

Dry cell batteries, on the other hand, are light and compact. Commonly used in flashlights and portable cassette players, dry cell batteries produce their energy through a reaction between a metal rod and a dry powder. Voltage produced by a single dry cell ranges from 1.5–9 volts. When connected in series, dry cells can be used to power small lighting fixtures. Standard zinc and alkaline dry cells may not be used again once their power is depleted; nickel-cadmium batteries, however, are rechargeable.

The *generator* is the most commonly used source of power for big location shoots and the direct current it produces is much safer than household AC. Generators come in many sizes, produce 40–2000 amps of current, and many provide AC as well as DC.

Because DC is impractical for long-distance transmission, electricity is supplied by the power company as AC. In the United States, AC changes direction in a circuit 120 times a second (60 Hertz).

CIRCUITS

Power is furnished to most buildings by the supply company at a nominal 240 volts, cabled in at the main box. This 240 volts AC (VAC) is divided into one or two circuits of 240VAC (to power appliances such as stoves or washers) and several more of less hazardous 120-VAC circuits.

Most modern houses in the United States have a current supply of 100 amps. The power is divided into several circuits, each with its own amperage limit of 20 (but sometimes 15 or 30) amps each. Each circuit may go to a different part of the house and outlets in large rooms may be on two or more separate circuits.

It is important to find out which outlets are connected to which circuits. Suppose you are going to light a living room, which has outlets on two circuits of 20 amps each. You need to find out which outlets are on which circuits as well as the maximum wattage you may draw from each circuit. This may be derived from the following equation:

$$\text{watts} = \text{volts} \times \text{amperes}$$

or

$$\frac{\text{watts}}{\text{volts}} = \text{amperes}$$

Many gaffers and electricians memorize this formula by using the phrase "*West VirginiA.*"

In practice, voltage may vary between 110 and 120, and may be rounded off to 100 (for a margin of safety). You also know that each circuit is wired for 20 amps. When you multiply the known volts by the known amps, you'll find that

$$100 \text{ volts} \times 20 \text{ amps} = 2000 \text{ watts}$$

Therefore, you may use lamps that draw a combined total of no more than 2000 watts per circuit.

FUSES AND CIRCUIT BREAKERS

If you try to draw more than 20 amps from a 20-amp circuit, the increased load will blow a fuse or circuit breaker in the main box. Fuses and circuit breakers are safety devices designed to stop the flow of current if a circuit becomes overloaded. When the amperage drawn on the circuit exceeds the safe capacity of the wiring in the circuit, the result is increased resistance and heat. If allowed to go unchecked, the heat may melt the wiring.

A *fuse* contains a piece of metal that melts at a temperature far below the melting point of circuit wiring. When a circuit is overloaded, the metal will melt and break the circuit. Fuses may be one of two kinds—cartridge or screw-mount (see Figure 3.3)—and are rated according to the amperage they allow. When a fuse blows, it must be replaced to restore power to a circuit. Conductive materials such as copper pennies should never be inserted in a socket in place of a fuse

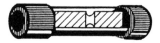

FIGURE 3.3 Cartridge and screw-mount fuses.

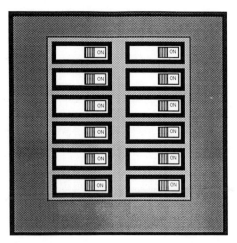

FIGURE 3.4 Circuit breakers in a main box panel.

because they will not limit the amperage to prevent an overload.

Most modern buildings use the more convenient *circuit breakers* to perform the same function as a fuse. Circuit breakers are more convenient as they may be reset at the circuit box simply by flipping a switch (see Figure 3.4).

Even when wall current is readily available, professional production crews often use big generators to supply power to lighting equipment. Low-budget filmmakers who are unable to afford generators, on the other hand, may seek to avoid the bother of isolating and plugging into standard circuits and, instead, resort to hazardous power tie-ins. A tie-in involves bypassing the main circuit breaker box and connecting a portable distribution box directly to the main power cable, which carries 220 or sometimes 440 VAC. A tie-in is generally implemented to centralize the power distribution.

Tie-ins are a risky practice at best and are prohibited by law in many areas. The safe alternatives to tie-ins are to plug in to available circuits or use generators.

RESISTANCE, VOLTAGE DROP, AND COLOR TEMPERATURE

The product of resistance is heat. A tungsten lamp filament resists current and becomes hot when it emits light. In the same way, a copper wire that is too thin for the load it carries also becomes hot—a fire hazard. Safe power distribution requires electrical cables of the proper thickness or gauge.

When the distance between the electrical source and the load is too great, increased resistance creates *voltage drop*. Voltage drop (vd) is determined by wire gauge and length, and is equal to current times resistance (vd = c × r). Usually, the margin of safety afforded by assuming a circuit supports 100-volts allows for any potential voltage drop.

Wire gauge is designated by a number; the lower the number, the larger the diameter of the wire. The largest wire gauge used in film and video lighting is no. 0000 (four aught), while the smallest size is no. 18. The standard thickness for a 2000 watt lamp is 12 gauge. As a rule, the larger the diameter of a wire, the more amperage it can safely carry.

The lamps of any lighting instrument are designed to produce light of a given color temperature only when the right amount of voltage reaches the bulbs (usually 115–120 volts). As the voltage drops, the Kelvin rating decreases. A voltage drop of 10 volts will cause a 100°K drop in color temperature.

CABLES AND CONNECTORS

Wires and cables are generally made of two or three insulated wires encased in a rubber or plastic sleeve. The *hot wire*, which is color-coded black, carries electricity to the load from the source. The black wire is the wire that is broken for the on/off switch of a fixture or circuit. The green, *ground wire* carries electricity to the earth in the event of a short. The white, *neutral wire* takes the current back to the source to complete the circuit (see Figure 3.5).

Avoid using two-wire cable in lighting applications. Should a broken wire touch a lamp housing or other exposed conductor, the current in the wire will travel the path of least

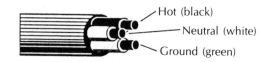

FIGURE 3.5 Cross-section of a grounded cable.

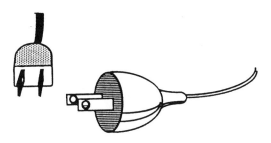

FIGURE 3.6 Common, two-blade household plugs.

FIGURE 3.7 Three-prong (tri-edison) plug.

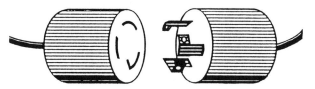

FIGURE 3.8 Twist-lock connectors.

FIGURE 3.9 Three-pin connector.

resistance and create a short. Beware! Should someone be unfortunate enough to touch the fixture, alternating current will be conducted through their body and could grab and hold the person to the fixture. A steady flow of electricity through a body may cause heart failure.

There are a number of different cable connectors and they should always be checked for compatibility with each other and with AC cables, extension cords, and all the other distribution equipment. *Plugs* are male connectors that join the cable to the female receptacle or socket. Although there are many types of plugs and receptacles, those most often encountered by the location filmmaker are the standard household, the three-prong household, and the twist-lock plugs.

Commonly known as *standard household plugs*, these plastic, two-blade connectors (see Figure 3.6) are usually rated at 15 amps. Household plugs are found in many thin-gauge extension cords and at the end of most wires leading from lamps. Don't use such an extension cord for a grounded fixture; use a suitable gauge cord with a three-prong plug instead.

Also called *heavy-duty plugs, three-prong connectors* always have two, parallel, flat blades and a third ground prong (see Figure 3.7). Besides offering a grounded connection, they can usually handle a current of up to 30 amps.

Twist-lock plugs have replaced most other plugs in studio applications. The locking feature prevents disconnection due to cable tension and the circular blade configuration prevents the ground wire from being bypassed or broken (see Figure 3.8). The twist-lock connector is found on practically all ellipsoidal fixtures and on most other fixtures used exclusively in studios and theaters.

Three-pin connectors (see Figure 3.9) are often associated with cables that supply power to instruments that draw a lot of current, such as arc lamps and hydrargyrum medium-arc length iodide (HMI) lamps. These plugs can be pulled apart when they are placed under stress. In older theaters, *stage plugs* (or paddles) are still used. This flat, bladelike connector is outmoded and unsafe, and should only be handled by an electrician.

Self-Study

■ QUESTIONS

1. If you know a fixture has a 2000-watt lamp and you round off the available voltage to 100W, you can easily figure that the lamp will draw no more than _____ amps of current.
   a. 20
   b. 2
   c. 12
2. A buildup of resistance in long power cables can lead to _____, resulting in color temperature changes.

a. voltage drop
b. static cling
c. amping out

3. The electrical current available in a typical American household is divided into several circuits, each of which provides _____.
a. 50 Hertz
b. 15–20 amperes
c. 220–240 volts
d. 50,000 watts

4. Voltage is a measure of electrical _____.
a. current
b. potential
c. power
d. resistance

5. American electrical current alternates at _____.
a. 50 Hz
b. 60 Hz
c. 1000 Hz
d. 400–700 nanometers

6. How many 5K lamps can one plug into a standard household circuit before blowing a fuse or circuit breaker?

7. Voltage drop is equal to current times _____.
a. power
b. potential
c. resistance
d. luminance

8. How many 650-watt lamps can be plugged into a 20-amp house circuit before a fuse or circuit breaker blows?

9. An 18-gauge, AC cord can carry greater amounts of current more safely than a 12-gauge, AC cord.—True or false? _____.

10. The safest electrical connector is the _____.
a. stage plug
b. household plug
c. three-prong plug
d. twist-lock plug

■ ANSWERS

1. **a.** Remember that total amperage equals total wattage of all fixtures used divided by the voltage of the circuit (A = W/V). Since actual household voltage may fluctuate between 105 and 120 volts, it is customary to round that figure to 100 volts, which also allows for a margin of safety. Thus, 2000 watts divided by 100 volts equals 20 amps of current.

2. **a.** Resistance is the opposition offered by a body to passage of an electric current. Resistance may result in heat buildup and a decrease in voltage equal the amount of resistance in the line. Voltage drop may be alleviated by shortening the distance between the power source and the instruments, using wider gauge cable, or both.

3. **b.** Current, or electrical flow, is measured in amps. An average house may have a total of 100 amps available, which are split into several circuits of 15–20 amps each. Voltage is a measure of electromotive force or pressure and is supplied by the power company at 220–230VAC at the main box, and is split into several circuits of 110 volts each. Wattage is a measure of electrical power consumed by lamps and other appliances. Hertz refers to the cycles per second of alternating current.

4. **b.** Voltage is a measure of electromotive force or potential. See answer to #3.

5. **b.** In the United States, electrical current alternates at 60 Hz, while in Europe the standard is 50 Hz. (This partly explains the difference in television standards on both continents.)

6. The answer is none. A 5 Kilowatt lamp consumes 5000 watts of electricity, which when divided by 100 volts

equals 50 amps. This amperage exceeds the current amperage allotment of an average household circuit by more than a factor of two and would certainly result in a blown circuit breaker or fuse. The only way to supply power to such a high-watt instrument is to find and use a 50-amp or more circuit, or use a generator.

7. c. Voltage drop is equal to current times resistance.

8. A total of three 650-watt fixtures may be used for a total of 1950 watts. If $A = W/V$, then $W = A \times V$. We know the maximum current available is 20 amps and the voltage will always be 100; thus, we may use a total of 2000 watts (or three 650-watt fixtures).

9. false. Gauge numbering increases as cable thickness decreases. While 18 gauge is sufficient for a low-watt desk lamp or radio, 12 gauge is considered adequate for a 1000-watt lighting fixture.

10. d. The twist-lock plug has a ground connection that cannot be bypassed and forms a connection that cannot be easily pulled apart, thus making it the safest connector. The stage plug, with exposed copper banding, is perhaps the most hazardous connector still in use. The standard, two-blade household plug contains no provision for grounding a possible short circuit and thus is unsafe for any power loads that exceed 100 watts. The three-prong household plug has a built-in ground pin that is too easily bypassed or cut off. Both connections may part easily unless they are tied or taped together.

■ PROJECT 3.1:   LOCATION PREVIEW—DETERMINING ELECTRICAL LOAD

Purpose:

To determine power availability in a given location.

Materials Needed:

assistant
notebook and pen or pencil
graph paper for drawing a floor plan
night light or small plug-in lamp

Procedure:

All buildings that have alternating current have a main box at which the electricity enters the building and is distributed. If possible, find the main box in your house or building and note its location and distribution system (which rooms the circuits are allocated to).

1. Do the circuits use fuses or circuit breakers?
2. If fuses are employed, are they screw-mount or cartridge fuses?
3. Are the various circuits labeled? Is it possible to tell where each circuit is connected and to which rooms they supply power? If not, determine how the circuits are distributed in the house or portion of the building you need to light. Accomplish this by plugging a night-light or small lamp into each outlet while an assistant tries the various circuits.
4. Note the presence of any high-watt appliances such as refrigerators, air conditioners, electrical heaters, dryers, washing machines, motors, etc. Try to determine their maximum wattage requirements and decide if they may be temporarily turned off or unplugged.
5. Draw a floor plan of the house or area you will be using, show the location of every outlet, and indicate which circuit controls each outlet. Label each circuit and its maximum amperage load. How many amps are available for lighting equipment?

CHAPTER FOUR

Video, the Electronic Medium

INTRODUCTION

Video and *television* are terms used to describe the electronic medium for gathering, recording, and transmitting moving images and sound. Video production has gradually transcended its broadcast radio beginnings and adopted many techniques used in location and studio filmmaking. Video is an inherently electronic medium, however, and differs from photographic film in many fundamental respects. Since it responds to light in a different way than film, it deserves to be considered in a separate category.

Video in the United States works on a system approved by the National Television Systems Committee (NTSC) in the early 1940s. In the NTSC system, a video picture is scanned as 60 fields per second, in agreement with the 60-Hz AC standard used in North America. A video picture is scanned and reproduced using 525 horizontal lines—a process known as *interlace*. Each complete frame is comprised of two separate fields of 262.5 lines. The pattern of lines that constitutes the scanning pattern is called *raster*.

VIDEO AND FILM COMPARED

Video technology differs from motion picture technology in several fundamental ways and these differences influence our overall perceptions about the "video look" versus the "film look." Videotape, originally developed as a medium for recording live television broadcasts and news events, now rivals film as a single-camera medium for originating dramatic as well as informational programming. Video origination, which emphasizes high production values, is called *electronic field production* (EFP). Informational, interview, documentary, and news material shot with portable video equipment is known as *electronic news gathering* (ENG). Lighting for video production becomes much more dependent on the content and uses of the programming than on the nature of the medium itself. For instance, the immediacy or "live" look often attributed to video daytime drama and television news footage is largely a reaction to the often rudimentary lighting techniques used to produce such programming. Electronic production has become ever more sophisticated by adopting many film-lighting techniques and blurring many traditional differences between the two media.

VIDEO IMAGING

The video camera gathers and focuses a picture much like a film camera. Professional, color video cameras, however, use beam splitters (prisms that separate light into two or more paths) and dichroic (or color-separating) filters to split incoming white light into its three additive primaries—red, green, and blue. Pickup tubes or solid-state, charge-coupled devices (CCDs) in the camera capture the images.

The Pickup Tube

Pickup tube cameras are rapidly giving way to those using completely solid-state designs. Nonetheless, the pickup tube camera, which has been around since its perfection by Vladimir Zworykin, Philo Farnsworth, and others in the 1920s, is still widely used professionally.

Traditional tube cameras focus an image on a tissue-thin, metal screen located at the front end of a pickup tube (see Figures 4.1 and 4.2). When light strikes the photoelectric metal, electrons are bumped out of their orbits and knocked out of the screen. The electrons strike a metal plate, called the *video target*, located immediately behind the photoelectric screen. An electron gun at the other end of the pickup tube shoots a stream of electrons that sweeps across the target in a series of lines and scans the image much like the way that your eyes are scanning the lines of this text. The image formed on the target is the result of variances in the brightness levels across each of the 525 lines that comprise the video picture.

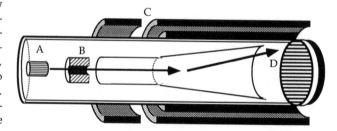

FIGURE 4.1 How the pickup tube forms an image. An electron beam emerges from an electron gun (A) and is pulled by an anode (B) as it passes through the tube. The magnet and coils (C) deflect the beam, causing it to scan the video target (D) in a zigzag pattern, thereby dissecting the image into lines.

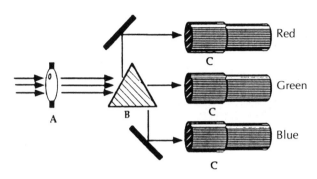

Red
Green
Blue

FIGURE 4.2 The three-tube video camera uses a beam-splitting prism, which splits light into its three primaries. The hues are directed by mirrors to red, green, and blue tubes, respectively. The green tube also carries luminance (light-dark) information. The separate signals are ultimately combined to form a composite video image.

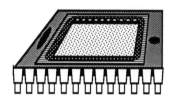

FIGURE 4.3 The charge-coupled device (or CCD). The CCD is a microprocessor chip that contains several hundred thousand photodiodes (pixels), which record an entire video image, rather than scan one line at a time, as does the pickup tube.

The problem with pickup tubes is the way in which they deal with overexposure. Image retention (or lag) may occur when a highlight from one image carries over into the next; this appears as a ghost image that is left by moving shapes. Specular highlights that move within a scene are apt to cause a distracting "comet-tail" effect, particularly at wider apertures, that can be seen as white smears that trail across the video image when reflective metallic objects or light sources (such as candles) move across the frame. Strong backlight is likely to cause *blooming*, which distorts both luminance and chrominance in the image.

The Charge-Coupled Device

Just as transistors have replaced vacuum tubes in amplifiers, so have solid-state sensors largely supplanted pickup tubes in video cameras. The prevalent design used in today's solid-state cameras is the CCD (or chip). The CCD does not scan the image with an electron beam as does the tube, but rather the sensor contains thousands of discrete picture elements (called *pixels*) that read the entire image at once (see Figure 4.3). Image resolution (or sharpness of detail) depends only on the number of pixels in a given chip. Since the image is composed of a mosaic of pixels, an image with very fine

detail is apt to cause a *moire*—a distracting, wavy line pattern that occurs with parallel line and grid patterns in the scene. The more pixels that can be squeezed onto the chip, the less likely this defect will occur.

Solid-state sensors are virtually impervious to lag, image burn (a lingering hot spot left on the screen by a specular highlight), and comet-tailing. CCDs are much more accurate than pickup tubes in their rendition of black and shadow areas. Therefore, a less noisy (i.e., a less grainy or snowy) image can be captured with solid-state sensors.

LIGHT LEVELS

Most video cameras are calibrated to have an effective EI of approximately 100. It is possible to increase a video camera's light sensitivity by "boosting the gain," which is similar to forced processing in film. The intensity of a video signal is measured in decibels (dB), rather than stops, as with film. A 6 dB increase doubles the effective EI to 200, and a 12 dB increase gives an effective EI of 400. However, increased gain results in a noisier picture and the problem of noise is compounded in post-production and worsens with each successive generation.

CONTRAST RATIO

A video image often appears to lack a three-dimensional quality when compared with the film image. This lack has been partly solved by adding a circuit that artificially enhances the edges of objects within the scene. Unfortunately, this adds to the contrast of the picture.

The big difference between film and video lighting arises from differences in the contrast ratio of the two media. Video cameras reproduce values with a contrast ratio of 32:1 (or 5 stops), while color negative film can handle a contrast ratio that exceeds 128:1 (or 7 stops). To create the same overall effect for a scene shot in video, it is necessary to lower the lighting ratio by using more fill light (a light that lightens shadowed areas). At a given exposure level, objects that would produce marginal shadow detail on film would not register any detail at all on video. For example, a high-contrast, exterior night scene may look fine on film, but will lose crucial detail and block up (go black without detail) completely when shot on video. The solution to this problem is to add more fill light to reduce the inherent contrast of the scene. Lighting for video often requires adapting to its limited tonal range.

THE WAVEFORM MONITOR

The most valuable tool a cinematographer can have when shooting video is the *waveform monitor*. This monitor immediately reveals more information about an image than one could possibly get from a film lab.

The waveform monitor is a graphic display of the video signal generated by a camera (see Figure 4.4). Essentially, the monitor plots a graph of the video signal amplitude (image brightness) over image position from left to right. The vertical axis of the monitor display is divided into a scale of 100 Institute of Radio Engineers (IRE) units; 20 IREs equal 1 stop of camera exposure. The waveform monitor displays the signal for one line of the picture or a composite of the signals for every line in the frame.

Zero on the IRE scale (or absolute black) represents the *blanking level*, which can be seen as the black bar that rolls up a screen when the vertical hold is out of adjustment. Reference black, the darkest possible value within the picture, should be set at 7.5 IRE and is called the *setup level* or *pedestal*. The setup level represents the darkest value a picture may have, but this does not mean every picture must contain picture elements of this value. Any signal that exceeds 100 IRE appears as white in the picture.

The portion of the video signal that normally measures −40 IRE is the *sync pulse*, which regulates the scanning and fielding rate. The portion of the video signal in the −20 to +20 IRE range beneath the picture information contains the *color burst*, which carries the chrominance (color) information.

The waveform monitor is a combination light meter and contrast indicator. The green smears on the monitor screen that fall between 7.5 and 100 IRE illustrate the brightness range of any given scene. The highest peak of the green trace represents the brightest highlight, while the lowest valley denotes the darkest shadow. The range covered reveals the contrast levels within a frame and how much latitude is available.

A video signal cannot exceed 100 units; if the highlight signal is pressed up at 100 IRE so that the signal peaks have their tops chopped off, the result is called *clipping*, a function of a circuit that eliminates any portion of a signal that exceeds 100 IRE, and results in glaring whites that have little detail. Clipping is analogous to overexposure in film.

Some video cameras have a *zebra indicator*, which superimposes a striped pattern over parts of the image that exceed 70 IRE. This is a useful indicator if a waveform monitor is not available. Many reflected highlights, including the *highlighted* side of a face, will reach 70 IRE or greater on a waveform monitor. If the zebra pattern appears over a wide area of the image, it indicates that the striped area is in danger of clipping.

In order to properly set video levels, it is helpful to have a standard image that includes a known range of tones; this is done using a standard gray scale (or chip chart). The scale used in setting up video cameras is the (EIA) gray scale—a nine-step scale with reflectance of 3.0%, 4.4%, 6.3%, 9.2%, 13.4%, 19.5%, 28.4%, 41.3%, and 60% (see Figure 4.5). The chip chart is reproduced on the waveform monitor screen as a series of discrete steps and encompasses a contrast range of 20 to 1, with a one-half stop difference between each adjacent chip.

With the new chip cameras and the advent of high-definition, widescreen television, the quality of video will continue to improve and rival (and likely replace) film as a medium of origination. Creative lighting will continue to play a major part in the visual media in whatever form they may take.

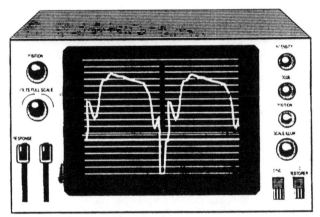

FIGURE 4.4 The waveform monitor. The portion of the signal approaching 100 IRE will appear white and the portion approaching 7.5 IRE will appear black; any part of the signal that exceeds 100 IRE will be clipped and may interfere with the video sync. The portion that dips to −40 IRE represents the syncing information.

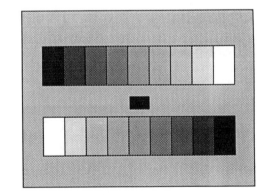

FIGURE 4.5 Standard EIA scale (chip chart).

Self-Study

■ QUESTIONS

1. The light-sensitive video counterpart to film emulsion is the _____.
   a. video target
   b. iron oxide
   c. videotape

2. The most accurate and helpful instrument for judging video lighting information is the _____ monitor.
   a. picture
   b. waveform
   c. vectorscope

3. The video image is limited to a contrast range of about 32 to 1 or _____ stops.
   a. 7
   b. 5
   c. 3

4. A video signal will register between 7.5 and 100 IRE on the waveform monitor screen. Any part of the signal that exceeds 100 IRE will be clipped and will register as _____ on a picture monitor.
   a. black
   b. white
   c. magenta

5. A doubling of video signal strength is equal to a one-stop increase in exposure and is measured on the waveform monitor screen in multiples of _____ IRE units.
   a. 1
   b. 5
   c. 20

6. The NTSC system used in the United States is based on a standard of _____.
   a. 16 fps
   b. 24 fps
   c. 30 fps

7. The NTSC system scans an image with _____ horizontal lines.
   a. 1125
   b. 625
   c. 525

8. The zebra pattern seen in some electronic displays usually occurs in the _____ range.
   a. 20-IRE
   b. 50-IRE
   c. 70-IRE

9. Large areas of strong backlight may cause video image _____.
   a. blooming
   b. comet-tailing
   c. poor tracking

10. The resolution of CCD devices is limited to the _____.
    a. size of pickup tube
    b. gauge of videotape
    c. number of pixels used

■   ANSWERS

   1. a. The light-sensitive video counterpart to film emulsion is the video target, which is the part of the camera on which the image is focused. The metallic coating of videotape records video (and audio) magnetically and is not sensitive to visible light.
   2. b. The waveform monitor gives instant information about video image contrast. The picture monitor, though easy to use, does not give an accurate indication of contrast and color, and may give misleading and inconsistent results. The vectorscope monitor is an instrument used primarily by engineers to adjust the hue of additive and subtractive primary colors.
   3. b. The video camera can reproduce a contrast ratio of about 32:1 or 5 stops. The average home television receiver can reproduce a somewhat reduced contrast ratio of roughly 20:1 or just over 4 stops. In comparison, photographic film can resolve about a 128:1 ratio or 7 stops.
   4. b. A video signal that exceeds 100 IRE on the waveform monitor will be clipped and is reproduced as white. Black values are represented as any part of the signal that dips below 7.5 IRE. Magenta and any other hues cannot be measured on a waveform monitor.
   5. c. The waveform monitor screen is divided into 100 IRE units. The equivalent of a one-stop increase (or doubling) in light intensity is a 20-IRE increase. Thus, the waveform monitor can read a video signal that is limited to 5 stops. If the signal exceeds 100 IRE, it will be clipped.
   6. c. The NTSC system is pegged to the standard alternating current rate in the United States—60 Hz. The video frame is made up of *two* interlacing fields, which occur 60 times per second. Thus, 30 fps occur, as opposed to the 24-fps film rate.
   7. c. The NTSC system dissects an image into 525 horizontally scanning lines.
   8. c. The zebra indicator lets the camera operator know how much and what portions of the image exceed 70 IRE. If these areas of high brightness predominate, the image may suffer from clipped highlights.
   9. a. The video image defect that occurs where edges of contrasting values meet is known as *blooming* and is caused when poorly illuminated subjects appear before very bright backgrounds. Comet-tailing, a related phenomenon, occurs when small specular highlights and sources cross the image and result in a smear of light. Poor tracking is an unrelated problem of videotape recorders.
   10. c. In video cameras, resolution depends on the number of minute parts into which the picture can be divided and reassembled. The image definition characteristics of CCD sensors is based on how many separate pixels can be squeezed onto the chip. The highest quality CCDs and pickup tubes boast more than 700 lines of image resolution, despite the fact that the NTSC system is limited to 525 lines. Gauge (or width) of the videotape is not a primary factor in video resolution as it is in film.

■ **PROJECT 4.1:   USING THE WAVEFORM MONITOR**

Purpose:

To gain experience with the waveform monitor.

Materials Needed:

waveform monitor
video camcorder or camera with VCR
video cables with compatible connectors
EIA gray scale (chip chart)
notebook and pen

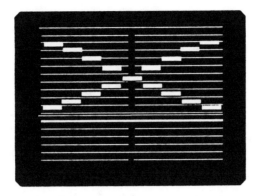

FIGURE 4.6 Waveform rendition of a nine-step chip chart at gamma 4.5.

Procedure:

1. Set up the video camera and waveform monitor, and set up the chip chart so that the camera takes in the entire chart in its viewfinder. If the video camera is set up on the chip chart so that the black chip is at 20 units on the waveform monitor and the white chip is at 100 units, then the middle-gray chip will fall at about 55 units, as illustrated in Figure 4-6.
2. Replace the chip chart with an 18% reflectance gray card and observe the signal on the chip chart. Now turn the card over to the 90% reflectance, white side. Note how the signal peaks at 100 IRE. Slowly close down the iris while watching the monitor and notice how the signal moves down the IRE scale.
3. Shoot a scene and identify and correlate the lightest and darkest areas of the scene with the IRE levels on the waveform monitor display. What are the brightest and darkest elements in the scene? Note the video level of each in IRE units.
4. If possible, set up a VHS VCR so that its signal can be seen on the waveform monitor display. Play a videocassette of any movie that includes both exterior, daytime and nighttime scenes; compare them on the monitor. How do the displays differ?

CHAPTER FIVE

Controlling Color Temperature: Light Sources and Filters

INTRODUCTION

The development of fast film emulsions, highly sensitive video cameras, and a wide array of improved lamps have freed the cinematographer from shooting exclusively by daylight. Today there are a wide range of options when it comes to selecting light sources for film and video production. The diversity of lamps and stock, however, bring up the problems of balancing and filtering sources of different color temperature.

COLOR TEMPERATURE

The eye is remarkably adaptive to color and perceives a variety of light sources as white light sources. The light from any given source, however, is dominated by certain wavelengths that determine its overall hue (or color) temperature. Film is designed to react correctly only to light sources with specific combinations of wavelengths. Panchromatic (black-and-white) film is overly sensitive to the blue portion of the spectrum, as illustrated in Figure 5.1. Hence, when outdoor scenes are photographed with panchromatic film, skies appear white and flesh-tone values appear dark, unless a filter is used in front of the camera lens. A *filter* is a colored sheet of glass or clear plastic that transmits its observable hue and absorbs all others. Yellow and red filters, which block blue hues, are the most popular with black-and-white photography.

The problem of color balance and temperature is more critical with color films. The same film that gives faithful results under incandescent light renders a scene blue under daylight. Conversely, a film that reproduces accurate color in sunlight records scenes in reddish orange tones under incandescent light. Thus, the cinematographer must always take into account two factors—the color temperature of the light source and the color balance of the film emulsion.

In contrast, the electronic circuitry of the video camera provides the videographer with the option of shooting color-corrected scenes under lighting conditions of differing color temperature, provided the camera is white-balanced (set up for the balance of ambient light) beforehand. The camera will correctly balance for any continuous spectrum source, thus eliminating filtering the camera lens.

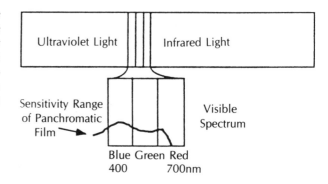

FIGURE 5.1 Normal photographic section of the electromagnetic spectrum showing the blue bias of panchromatic film.

The Kelvin Scale

Color temperature is measured according to a scale devised by Lord William Thompson Kelvin in the late nineteenth century. This scale measures the color temperature of a light source by comparing its light to that of a perfect black body (a theoretical carbon block that, at room temperature, reflects zero light). The black body is heated until it glows, much like a piece of iron in a fire. At low temperatures, the black body gives off a red glow; at higher temperatures, it gives off orange, yellow, and finally a blue hue. The temperature of the black body is taken when its color matches the light source. This temperature reading is taken in Celsius and then converted to Kelvin by adding 273° to the original measurement (0°C equals the freezing point of water, while 0°K equals −273°C—the point at which all molecular activity stops). The Kelvin system is accurate for measuring the color temperature of a source that generates its light through incandescence (glowing with heat). Sources that create light through fluorescence and discharge arc cannot be accurately measured in degrees Kelvin, because they do not emit all hues of the visible spectrum. The term *correlated color temperature* is used to describe the spectral energy distribution of these nonincandescent sources.

Variance of Color Temperature

Since film does not adapt to light variations as does the human eye, film manufacturers balance their emulsions for one of two general color temperatures—3200°K for interiors (tungsten) and 5500°K for exteriors (photographic daylight). For the sake of uniformity, most filmmakers use 3200°K-balanced film and filter the camera outdoors with a #85B orange filter, thereby matching the 5500°K daylight to the 3200°K emulsion. Because still photographers use tungsten sources less frequently, film for still photography is usually balanced for daylight.

Though film emulsions are balanced for either 3200°K or 5500°K only, the actual color temperature of different sources may vary widely. The deep blue sky may reflect light measuring as high as 30,000°K, compared to candlelight, which may measure a very warm 1900°K (see Figure 5.2).

PHOTOGRAPHIC DAYLIGHT

Daylight may vary in color temperature, depending on the time of day, the position of the sun, the presence or absence of clouds or smog, and other factors. Pure sunlight reaches the earth's atmosphere at about 6000°K–7000°K. As the light penetrates the air, the short wavelengths (blue and ultraviolet) are scattered. The filtered sunlight arrives at about 5400°K, while the atmosphere diffuses the blue wavelengths and radiates them back to earth as skylight, measuring between 10,000°K–25,000°K. The resulting overall color temperature depends on the ratio of sunlight to skylight. On a clear day at noon, skylight may comprise from 10%–20% of the total illumination, for a combined color temperature of 6100°K–6500°K.

As the sun approaches the horizon, the light slowly changes color from white to yellow to red, as the rays pass through thickening layers of atmosphere (see Figure 5.3). Dust and other particles in the air scatter much of the light, leaving only the long wavelengths (red) to penetrate to the earth's surface. At sunset, the color temperature of daylight may be somewhere around 2000°K, while twilight may be bluer than noontime daylight. Anytime a cloud passes over the sun, light will emanate from the blue sky, resulting in a color temperature that may exceed 15,000°K.

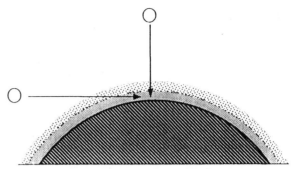

FIGURE 5.3 As the sun approaches the horizon, its light must penetrate increasing layers of atmosphere, which scatter the shortwave violet and blue rays, and give the sunset its familiar reddish cast.

FIGURE 5.4 Standard incandescent lamp.

TUNGSTEN ILLUMINATION

The primary artificial light source used in film and video production is the incandescent lamp, which comes in two forms—standard tungsten (incandescent) and tungsten-halogen.

Thomas Edison did not invent the incandescent light bulb, but he improved the design significantly so as to make it a practical lighting instrument for the home. Edison's lamp used a carbon filament that glowed too dimly to be of use to the infant motion picture industry in the late nineteenth century. The tungsten filament was perfected in 1909 and is far superior to the carbon filament, as it creates a much brighter light.

Standard Incandescent Lamps

The standard incandescent lamp has evolved very little since 1909 and consists of a coiled tungsten filament within a thin glass bulb or envelope (see Figure 5.4). The filament resists

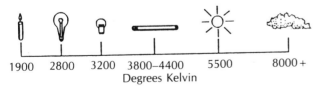

1900   2800   3200   3800–4400   5500   8000+
Degrees Kelvin

FIGURE 5.2 Variation of color temperature in common light sources, in degrees Kelvin.

the flow of electricity that passes through it, which causes the filament to heat up and glow. Nitrogen gas within the envelope prevents the filament from oxidizing. Electrical current is conducted through the base, which fits within the socket of a lighting fixture.

Household light bulbs are the most common example of the standard incandescent lamp. They are not very efficient sources in terms of the power they consume (measured in watts), compared to the actual amount of light they generate (measured in lumens). The standard measure of electric light efficiency is measured in lumens per watt. The average standard incandescent lamp's low wattage (10–250W), low efficiency (14–18 lumens per watt), and low color temperature (2900°K, when new) make it unsatisfactory for film and video work. The only standard incandescent lamp used professionally is the photoflood lamp, which is used primarily by portrait photographers. The photoflood, with a color temperature of 3400°K, is designed to be used with panchromatic and type A (balanced for 3400°K) color emulsions. The useful life span of the photoflood is limited, however, because the color temperature begins to drop after only a few hours of use.

Although standard incandescent bulbs may last from 750–1000 hours, color temperature drops as the lamp ages, due to a phenomenon known as *boil-off*. The lamp's filament glows at very high temperatures, causing tungsten molecules to boil off. The particles settle and cling to the inside of the envelope, creating a black deposit (see Figure 5.5). While this occurs, the filament thins, passes less current, and glows with diminishing intensity. The combination of these factors results in diminishing color temperature—the light gradually becomes weaker and more reddish with age. These shortcomings have been overcome with the advent of the tungsten-halogen lamp.

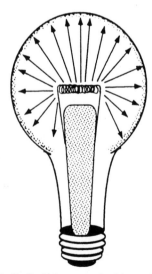

FIGURE 5.5 Boil-off in a standard incandescent lamp.

Tungsten-Halogen Lamps

In 1880, Edison suggested that if a halogen gas, such as iodine, was pumped into an incandescent lamp bulb, it would allow the tungsten element to glow at a temperature of at least 3000°C, thereby redepositing the boiled off particles back onto the filament. In order to facilitate the regenerative process, the envelope had to be extremely compact. Unfortunately, no silica glass could withstand such intense heat. In the 1950s, the General Electric Company developed a quartz glass that could withstand extreme temperatures; this advent made possible the tungsten-halogen (or quartz) lamp (see Figure 5.6).

Tungsten-halogen lamps have almost completely superseded the standard tungsten lamp in the film and television industries. Because the regenerative halogen gas is contained within the quartz envelope and redeposits tungsten particles back on the filament, the lamps do not blacken and change color with age. Tungsten-halogen lamps are designed to emit light of a great intensity—about 20 lumens per watt. Average bulb life is 4000 hours. Tungsten-halogen lamps used in the motion picture and television industries are generally designed to burn at a constant 3200°K.

Tungsten-halogen lamps have one distinct disadvantage—the intense light they give off is accompanied by extreme heat. Therefore, tungsten-halogen lamps must be kept a safe distance from drapes, painted walls, wood, and sprinkler systems.

Do not touch the quartz bulb of a tungsten-halogen lamp with your bare hands, even when it is cold. The oils deposited on the glass will create a hot spot on the bulb, causing it to crack and possibly explode. Handle bulbs with gloves or a towel. Vibration is the main enemy of tungsten filaments. Do not jiggle or shake them, particularly when they are hot.

FLUORESCENT LAMPS

The fluorescent lamp, a problematic source for the cinematographer, is discussed in this text because its very ubiquity has made it an unavoidable light source when shooting on location. Introduced by the General Electric Company in 1938, the fluorescent lamp has become the predominant lighting fixture in nearly all office buildings, schools, factories, and stores. The highly efficient fluorescent lamp can emit 40–80 lumens per watt over an average life span of 10,000 hours. As you will see, it is not a favorite light source of photographers or filmmakers; its peculiarities rate a discussion.

FIGURE 5.6 A tungsten-halogen lamp.

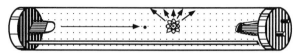

FIGURE 5.7 A standard fluorescent lamp. Electrodes at either end of the tube heat up as current passes through, emitting free electrons. The electrons strike atoms of mercury vapor in the tube, causing the atoms to give off ultraviolet (UV) radiation. The UV rays, in turn, strike a phosphorous coating on the inside of the tube, thereby stimulating the phosphors to emit visible light. This conversion of one kind of light into another is called fluorescence.

How the Fluorescent Lamp Works

A typical fluorescent lamp consists of a long glass tube that is sealed and has an electrical connection and filament at both ends (see Figure 5.7). The tube is coated on the inside with a mixture of fluorescent powders (called *phosphors*) and contains argon gas and a small amount of mercury. Electrical current passes through the filament and causes it to incandesce. The filament, called an *electrode*, emits electrons that shoot down the tube and collide with mercury atoms, which vaporize and fill the tube with mercury gas. The electrons bombard the mercury atoms, which give off ultraviolet radiation. This radiation stimulates the phosphors to give off visible light in certain wavelengths.

The fluorescent lamp requires alternating current to operate; thus the incandescent process reverses twice every cycle of AC current (or 120 times per second). This fluctuation is responsible for the phenomenon known as *strobing* or *flicker* and it may cause a pronounced effect on motion picture film. A camera with a shutter angle of less than 180° is more susceptible to strobing than one with a wider angle. Thus, flicker is likely to occur in film that is shot with a spring-wound or variable-speed camera, such as a Bolex H16, rather than with a synchronous sound camera, such as an Arriflex SR. Flicker does not pose a problem in video as it does in film, because video equipment and fluorescent lamps are pegged to the same 60-Hz AC standard.

Color Temperature Problems

Incandescent lamps emit all the colors of visible light; they have a continuous spectrum, which may be represented on a graph as an unbroken line. These spectral energy distribution (SED) graphs are used by the lighting industry to describe the different color temperatures of various light sources.

Standard fluorescent lamps emit high radiation in one or more wavelengths, but they do not contain all the hues found in the spectrum. The dominant wavelengths will register as spikes on the graph (see Figure 5.8). These dominant wavelengths translate on color film as an unmistakable, overall greenish blue light, which is typical of fluorescent lighting.

In general, fluorescent light must be filtered in some way if one intends to mix it with tungsten lamps or daylight. The eye compensates for this lack of spectral continuity—film does not. To compound the problem, there are at least six types of fluorescent lamps, each of which emit different portions of the visible spectrum.

CARBON ARC LAMPS

The brightest and hardest artificial light source available is the carbon arc, which was invented by Sir Humphrey Davy in 1801. Originally used for lighting city squares, fairs, and outdoor exhibitions, the carbon arc lamp enabled early film crews to move their cameras into the studio. These lamps are frequently used as the searchlights that sweep the skies at grand openings and public events.

The carbon arc lamp produces its light when high-amperage direct current is applied to one or two carbon rods or electrodes within the lamp housing. A stream of electrons in the current forms a brilliant arc as it jumps a narrow gap between the two carbon rods. As the lamp burns, the feed rod oxidizes and must be continually adjusted (or *trimmed*).

The carbon arc lamp most frequently used for film and television work is the 225-amp brute. There is no lamp that can better simulate the intense light of the sun or the hard light of the moon. The correlated color temperature of a white flame, carbon arc lamp is 5800°K, which closely matches photographic daylight.

For all its advantages, the carbon arc lamp has some distinct limitations. A bulky and heavy fixture, the carbon arc lamp requires a DC generator for power. The typical carbon arc lamp requires a voltage of 72 volts, which is supplied by a resistive grid (or ballast) that converts the normal 120 volts DC provided by most generators, and requires a technician to continually trim and replace carbons every 40 minutes, thus making it an expensive lamp to operate.

ENCLOSED ARC LAMPS

The most revolutionary artificial light source to be developed in recent years uses an enclosed arc lamp, which incorporates a medium-length mercury arc that is augmented with metal halides to alter the color of the emitted light. Enclosed arc lamps operate on alternating current only and require a high-voltage starter and a ballast to limit the current. Like fluorescent lamps, they exhibit a flickering that is noticeable on film if the illumination fades or decays too rapidly with each change in AC polarity. Enclosed arc lamps include the HMI, the compact iodide daylight (CID), the compact source iodide (CSI), and the industrial mercury and sodium discharge lamps.

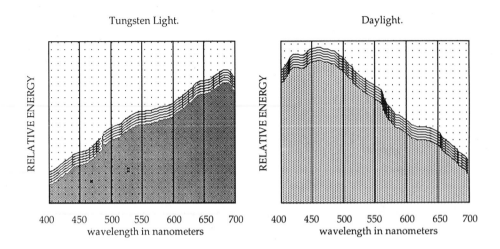

Tungsten Light.

Daylight.

Fluorescent Light.

FIGURE 5.8 Spectral energy distribution of tungsten lamps, daylight, and fluorescent lamps.

HMI Lamps

The *HMI lamp* is the most widely used, enclosed arc lamp for motion picture and television lighting. Instead of a filament, the HMI lamp incorporates a sealed arc within a bulb filled with mercury vapor and metal iodides (see Figure 5.9). The great advantage of the HMI lamp is its tremendous efficiency, which is usually expressed in lumens per watt of light. An Osram HMI 2500-watt bulb can produce 240,000 lumens of light, compared to a standard 2000-watt quartz bulb output of 50,000 lumens. This means that the HMI lamp can provide roughly four times as much light for the same amount of power required. Furthermore, the HMI lamp produces roughly half the heat generated by a similar tungsten lamp. Unlike the 3200°K tungsten lamp, the HMI lamp produces highly consistent, 5500°K illumination.

Because of their high efficiency and daylight balance, HMI lamps are used frequently for exterior applications,

FIGURE 5.9 An HMI lamp. Light is created when current arcs between the two electrodes.

largely supplanting the power-devouring carbon arcs. HMIs are particularly useful for filling in shadows outdoors and for supplementing daylight in interiors, and are a much better alternative than filtering tungsten lamps.

CID lamps also provide 5500°K illumination. CSI lamps provide light at 4200°K, which is readily filtered to either tungsten or daylight. CID and CSI lamps, though popular in Europe, are not used widely in the United States.

Metal iodide sources have some notable disadvantages. The HMI lamp is a heavy piece of hardware—the head weighs 60 pounds and the ballast adds an extra 145 pounds, for a total of 205 pounds. The fixtures are also very expensive; a 2500-watt lamp may well cost more than four 2000-watt tungsten lamps. Like the fluorescent lamp, the HMI lamp pulses at a rate equal to double the AC frequency (60Hz in the United States), resulting in flicker at a rate of 120 times per second. While this is of no concern to the videographer, the cinematographer will find that if the motion picture camera shutter is not synchronized with the 60-Hertz frequency, a noticeable strobing will result in the footage. Synchronization between shutter and lamp must be an even multiple of the 60-Hertz pulse rate. Thus, the standard 180° shutter found in most cameras will not perform satisfactorily. The camera speed must also be constant, through crystal sync or AC camera motors. These sync problems have been mitigated by means of a reduced decay flux in the newer lamps. Thus, flicker can almost be eliminated.

Industrial Discharge Lamps

Recent years have seen the increased use of discharge lamps in streetlights, stadiums, shopping malls, parking lots, and industrial sites. Thus, the cinematographer is certain to encounter this type of lighting at some time when shooting on location. Discharge lamps, which exhibit high efficiency (more than 100 lumens per watt) as well as odd-colored hard illumination, include mercury vapor and sodium lamps.

The clear mercury vapor lamp produces light that lacks red, blue, and blue-green wavelengths. It is impossible to add color where none exists, therefore no amount of filtration will transmit the absent hues. The only way to compensate for this deficiency is to overpower the mercury vapor light with continuous spectrum illumination, such as tungsten lighting.

Some mercury lamps have a phosphorous coating on the inside of the envelope, much like fluorescent lights. These lamps, known as *color-improved mercury vapor lamps*, have a more complete spectral energy distribution and are becoming more common in interior lighting situations.

High-pressure sodium lamps are used to illuminate boulevards and parking lots. Because they emit light primarily in the yellow wavelengths, they are easily recognized by their familiar orange-yellow color. Low-pressure sodium lamps, used widely in Europe, exhibit a similar, amber-colored light. No amount of filtering can even out the spectrum of low-pressure sodium lamps.

FILTERS

Filters modify light by transmitting only a portion of the light they receive. They can be used to create special effects, vary the tonal renditions of a scene, or adjust the color temperature and dominant color of light. As most filters absorb some of the light passing through them, they vary in their transmittance, expressed as a percentage (in lighting gels) or as a filter factor (in camera filters). The filter factor is expressed as the number of times exposure must be increased to compensate for light absorption. A doubling of exposure equals a one-stop increase. Thus, a filter factor of three would indicate an exposure increase of 1.5 stops.

Camera lens filters are usually made of glass or acetate. Expendable light source filters, made of acetate or polyester, are called *gels*, as they were formerly made of fragile gelatin. It should be noted that gels used for lighting are not optically clear enough to be used on camera lenses. As a rule, the thinner the filter, the less it will affect the performance of the lens.

Filters are made by a number of manufacturers. Camera filters are available from Eastman Kodak, Tiffen, and Harrison and Harrison. Rosco Laboratories offers a wide variety of gels for lighting. Manufacturers often have different names for the same filters. For example, the MT2, the CTO, and the #85 all refer to the same color-balancing amber filter used to convert daylight to tungsten.

General Purpose Filters

Ultraviolet (UV) filters are often used on camera lenses to cut haze in distant landscape shots. Because they absorb little visible light, they are often left in place at all times as a lens protector. UV filters are also used with arc, HMI, and sometimes fluorescent lamps to cut out the UV radiation emitted by those light sources.

The *polarizing filter* is used to reduce or eliminate reflections from glossy surfaces, such as glass and water, to increase color saturation and to darken the sky in landscape photography. Light, which normally vibrates in all directions at right angles to the direction of its propagation, is polarized when it is reflected by a glassy surface. The polarizing filter acts like a grill, blocking all but the light vibrating in a single plane.

Neutral density (ND) filters allow for the use of a wider lens aperture by cutting down the amount of light passing through the lens. This feature is particularly useful when using fast films on bright, exterior locations. ND filters do not conform to standard filter factors. They are, instead, calibrated in one-third-stop increments. An ND3, for example, cuts light by 1 stop. ND filters are often combined with other filters such as #85s.

Graduated filters are composed of a neutral density (or other color, such as rose) filter that gradually modulates to clear glass or acrylic. These filters are used for dramatic sky darkening and find wide use in music videos, commercial spots, and feature films.

Low-contrast filters, diffusion filters, fog filters, and *sheer fabric filters* such as gauze, all soften contrast and image definition in varying degrees. They are usually used to impart an impressionistic or dreamlike quality to a scene.

Color-Balancing Filters

In general, still photographers who work primarily with daylight and electronic flash use color film that is balanced for 5500°K. Because it is simpler to filter daylight than tungsten light, the cinematographer usually opts for a tungsten-balanced stock for maximum flexibility. The filmmaker usually wants grain, contrast, and color uniformity; this is ensured by purchasing film stock of the same batch.

Because the eye tends to adapt to the color temperature of a given source, it prevents an objective evaluation of a scene's color reproduction on film. Therefore, a color temperature meter is often used to judge the true color of the light in question. When the meter is pointed directly at a light source, it tells the color temperature in degrees Kelvin along with the color and amount of filtration needed to bring the light up to the desired color temperature.

When daylight and tungsten light are used simultaneously, one source is usually filtered to match the other. Daylight is always more intense than tungsten light, so it is more efficient to filter daylight using tungsten film in outdoor situations than it is to do the opposite. Daylight is converted to 3200°K with a Wratten #85 series filter; tungsten is converted to 5500°K with a Wratten #80 series filter. A #80 filter typically transmits half the light that a #85 transmits.

Contemporary cinematographers enjoy a great deal of freedom and regularly depart from strict adherence to 3200°K color temperature norms in order to create a more evocative image. The trend in recent years has been toward a warmer, more orange light for everyday situations. To this end, lights are often covered with orange or amber gels, like the traditional #54, the CTO, and the Rosco MT series.

Filtering Fluorescent Lamps

As noted earlier, fluorescent lamps present color-balancing problems when used in production. Unfortunately, it is often impossible to replace existing fluorescent lights on location. Therefore, the fixtures are sometimes left unfiltered for greater realism. Video cameras can be color balanced for fluorescent lamps, providing there is no tungsten light source in the scene. When filtering is called for, conversion gels and color-compensating filters may be used.

A scene lit entirely by fluorescent light can be filtered at the camera lens. In general, fluorescent light may be converted to 5500°K by using a CC30 magenta filter or converted to 3200°K with a combination of yellow and magenta filters. Another way to filter fluorescent light at the camera lens is to use a *FL*uorescent to *D*aylight emulsion (FLD) or *FL*uorescent to "*B*" type emulsions (3200°K) (FLB) filter. The FLB filter corrects warm fluorescent light, while the FLD filter corrects the daylight variety.

Usually, existing fluorescent lights must be augmented with more light. The idea is to create a balanced illumination of uniform color temperature. If windows (i.e., natural lighting) allow a large amount of daylight and the lamps are fluorescent daylight or cool white, the windows can be fil-

tered with a green gel, such as Tough Plusgreen/Windowgreen (Rosco Laboratories) to balance illumination. If tungsten sources are also used, they need to be filtered with Tough Plusgreen 50 (Rosco Laboratories). If 5000°K lamps, like FAY lights, are used as well, they should be treated as daylight and filtered with Tough Plusgreen/Windowgreen (Rosco Laboratories).

Sometimes it is more convenient to filter the fluorescent lamps themselves. In this case, magenta filters such as Tough Minusgreen (Rosco Laboratories), available in sheets or tube sleeves, are used. Don't be fooled by the resultant sickly purple illumination—it closely approximates 5500°K light. There are certain fluorescent tubes that eliminate filtering, such as the daylight-balanced Chroma 50 (General Electric) and the tungsten-matching Deluxe Warm White (General Electric).

Even though it is possible to have the lab timer correct for fluorescent light, it is best to correct as much as possible in production. The timer cannot correct different sources selectively; only the overall color can be adjusted. Too much correction in timing may boost contrast, grain, or both.

Filtering Arc-Type Lamps

The correlated color temperatures of white and yellow flame carbon arc lamps are rated at 5800°K and 3350°K, respectively. Therefore, some filtering is necessary to match arc light with daylight and tungsten standards.

The Y-1, a pale yellow filter, is commonly used with white flame carbons to match daylight; its transmission is rated at 90%. When it is desirable to match tungsten sources, a Y-1 plus an MT-2 (or #85B) is needed to provide 3200°K illumination. An MT-Y conveniently combines the Y-1 and MT-2 into one filter. Yellow flame carbon light may be converted to 3200°K with YF-101 filters. Other filters in the MT and CTO family may be used as necessary to warm the carbon arc light in varying degrees.

HMI lamps emit very high amounts of UV radiation, which may cause severe sunburn and possible eye damage in subjects. Therefore, HMI fixtures are fitted with special UV filter lenses. *Under no circumstances should an HMI lamp be altered to operate without this lens.* Although HMI lamps are designed to match daylight, they may vary in their correlated color temperature according to manufacturer and age, so it is best to use a color temperature meter to determine the amount of filtration needed. The Rosco Jungle Book, a 3-inch square booklet of color-compensating and color-balancing filters available free from Rosco Laboratories, is ideal for figuring proper filtration of light sources when used with a color temperature meter. Photographers also find the Jungle Book handy for trying various filters over a camera lens when testing a given film emulsion under illumination of unknown color temperature. For a complete summary of color-balancing and color-correcting filters, see Appendix A at the back of this book.

Self-Study

■ QUESTIONS

1. Boil off occurs as _____ lamps age.
   a. carbon arc
   b. HMI
   c. standard incandescent
2. Incandescence results when a filament _____ electricity.
   a. conducts
   b. resists
   c. polarizes
3. Photographic daylight measures _____ .
   a. 3200°K
   b. 5500°K
   c. 2900°K
4. Tungsten sources can be cooled to 5500°K by filtering with _____ gels.
   a. Minusgreen
   b. Tough Blue
   c. CTO
5. HMI lamps are often preferred to tungsten-halogen lamps because _____ .
   a. they are less expensive fixtures
   b. they are lightweight and compact
   c. they produce more light per watt use
6. Match the items on the left with the choices on the right.
   ____ Minusgreen (magenta)   a. converts daylight/tungsten film
   ____ #80A (blue)   b. converts tungsten light/daylight film
   ____ K2 (yellow)   c. fluorescent light/daylight film
   ____ #85B (amber)   d. corrects black-and-white film blue bias
   ____ Plusgreen (blue-green)   e. converts tungsten light to fluorescent light

■ ANSWERS

1. **c.** Although oxidation progressively shortens the life of arc lamps with use, tungsten filament boil off is a phenomenon peculiar to standard incandescent lamps.
2. **b.** Incandescence takes place when a tungsten filament resists electron flow.
3. **b.** Photographic daylight, a standard for balancing daylight emulsions, measures 5000°K. Tungsten-halogen lamps for film and television lighting are rated at 3200°K. Standard tungsten lamps average 2900°K.
4. **b.** Tough Blue filters will boost the color temperature of tungsten-halogen lamps to 5500°K. For this reason they are referred to as *booster blue*. Minusgreen, a magenta filter, is used as a color-compensating filter to match fluorescent light with daylight film. CTO is used to warm 5500°K daylight for balance with tungsten lamps.
5. **c.** While HMI lamps are much more expensive than tungsten-halogen lamps, and the ballast they require to operate is heavy and cumbersome to transport, they are, however, much more efficient in their lumens-per-watt output. HMI lamps average three to four times as much luminous intensity as a quartz lamp of similar wattage and they are cooler burning, too.
6. **c.,b.,d.,a.,e.** Minusgreen (magenta) is used for fluorescent light/daylight film combinations. #80A (blue) is used to convert tungsten light (3200°K) to match photographic daylight (5500°K). K2 (yellow) is used to correct the blue bias of panchromatic film. #85B (amber) is commonly used to convert daylight to tungsten film. Plusgreen (blue-green) converts tungsten-halogen light to fluorescent light.

■ PROJECT 5.1: IDENTIFYING ARTIFICIAL SOURCES

Purpose:

To gain familiarity with the design, function, and features of the various artificial sources available.

Materials Needed:

one new, standard incandescent light bulb
one old, standard incandescent light bulb
a tungsten-halogen lamp
a fluorescent lamp
a discharge-type light

Procedure:

Without looking directly at the lamps, observe each of them in operation, noting the differences in heat output, color temperature, and noise generated. Note the differences among the various lamp designs.

1. Compare the old, standard incandescent light bulb that has been in use with the new bulb.
2. Examine the tungsten-halogen lamp; be careful not to touch it with your bare hands. Note the compact envelope and the heavy, coiled filament.
3. Observe the fluorescent lamp while turning it on and off. Note how the lamp does not immediately come to full intensity like the incandescent lamps. Can you detect the strobing? Does the lamp emit any noise when it is on? What kind of noise is it? What causes it?
4. Look at the light given off by the discharge-type lamp. What wavelengths of light or hues are predominant? (Look at something of a known hue, such as a flag, to best gauge the cast.) Based on the perceived cast of the light, what type of lamp do you suppose it is? Mercury vapor? High- or low-pressure sodium?

■ PROJECT 5.2: USING COLOR-BALANCING AND COLOR-COMPENSATING FILTERS

Purpose:

To identify and correct the color temperatures of various light sources.

Materials Needed:

35 mm (SLR) camera with a through-the-lens (TTL) metering system
tripod
one roll Ektachrome 160 (tungsten-balanced)
Rosco Laboratories Jungle Book (available free from Rosco Laboratories, Inc.; 36 Bush Avenue; Port Chester, NY; 10573 or 1135 North Highland Avenue; Hollywood, CA; 90038)
camera log (see Figure 5.10)

Procedure:

Shoot a series of photographs, each framing a person in medium shot (including head and shoulders), as follows:

1. Take the first exposure in each group without a filter; then choose a different filter for each subsequent picture, holding the gels over the lens (either by hand or by holding it in place with tape). Use the most obvious filter

CAMERA LOG	PROJECT				FILM TYPE:	
EXPOSURE.	GROUP #	F/STOP	SH. SPD.	FILTER USED	LIGHT RATIO	SHOT DESCRIPTION

FIGURE 5.10 Camera log.

choices in order to correct the color balance. For example, daylight must be filtered to match tungsten film. Thus, a warming, amber-colored filter in the CTO series would be the logical choice in this instance. Try for a perfectly corrected and properly exposed scene in each group. Don't mix light sources of different color temperature in the same shot. For each exposure note the f-stop, shutter speed, lighting conditions, type of filter (if any) used, and a short description of the subject in the camera log. Circle the exposure you think uses the proper filter for the ambient light of the scene.

2. For Group A, exposures 1–5, photograph outdoors in daylight.
3. For Group B, exposures 6–10, photograph indoors under standard incandescent household bulbs.
4. For Group C, exposures 11–15, photograph indoors under fluorescent light.

5. For Group D, exposures 16–24, photograph a night scene outdoors under sodium or mercury vapor light (frequently found in parking lots of business and industrial locations). You need a tripod and you will need to shoot a variety of exposures to ensure at least one picture is shot with the proper exposure (e.g., f-2, f-2–2.8, f-2.8, etc.). At least one exposure in each set should be of a fully color-corrected scene.

Evaluating the Results:

View the processed slides with a projector if possible; compare the images within each lighting group and with the data you recorded in the camera log.

For Group A, the color temperature should be corrected if you used filters in the CTO or #85 (amber) series. Note the very subtle differences between each exposure; often, the correct filter will be a half or quarter CTO for the optimal desired effect.

For Group B, it is not usually necessary to correct tungsten light for tungsten film under normal circumstances. Standard incandescent lamps often need to be filtered in order to boost their color temperature to 3200°K. In this case, a third or quarter blue will boost color temperature 600° or 300°, respectively, and will provide the most accurate correction.

For Group C, color-balancing filters are used for boosting and decreasing color temperature in degrees Kelvin. In order to correct the light emitted by fluorescent and other discharge lamps, however, it is necessary to use color-compensating (CC) filters. The most useful CC filters for fluorescent correction are the magenta and green filters. Magenta is used to make fluorescent light compatible with 3200°K film, while green filters are used to match daylight sources, such as windows, to fluorescent lights. Therefore, filters of the Minusgreen or magenta series are the most logical choice.

For Group D, industrial discharge sources present the biggest challenge to the photographer. Sodium lamps are often difficult to correct, while mercury vapor lamps are virtually impossible to fully correct. Often, the best thing to do when faced with industrial lighting is to try to determine its overall cast, be it green, amber, or magenta, and then filter it with the closest complementary filter.

Compare your selections with the solutions above. Were your predictions about filtration accurate?

Controlling Light Quality: Lighting Equipment

INTRODUCTION

Every light source, whether it be the sun, sky, desk lamp, streetlight, fluorescent tube, candle, or professional lighting instrument, has its own character or quality. Color temperature has much to do with the inherent quality of a given source. However, the most important indication of the quality of light has to do with how it looks on a given subject. A picture of a subject taken outdoors under an overcast sky looks quite different from a picture of the same subject on a sunny day. An open window casts light of a distinctly different quality than that of an overhead fixture.

LIGHT QUALITY

This difference in quality affects the nature of shadows cast on the subject and background; they will appear hard or soft, depending on the quality of the light source. The hardness or softness of shadows cast by any light source is dependent on two factors—distance between the subject and the source, and the size of the light source.

All other things being equal, when the *distance* between the subject and the background is increased, the shadow softens. In most shooting situations, the relationships between subjects cannot always be altered (e.g., the relationship between a subject's nose and face). Therefore, the second factor becomes very important—*the size of the light source.*

Light sources with large areas from which the light emanates will cast soft shadows, while those with small areas will cast hard shadows (see Figure 6.1). The light from large sources, such as an overcast sky, tends to wrap around the subjects and fill in any cast shadows.

But because apparent size of source is more important than actual size when it comes to determining light quality, the distance from the light source to the subject is also a factor. When a lighting unit is very close to a given subject, the source is also relatively large. However, when the light is moved further away from the subject, the source becomes relatively small. A good example of a hard light source is the sun. Although it is actually the largest source available, its great distance makes it appear to be a small size source and hence very specular.

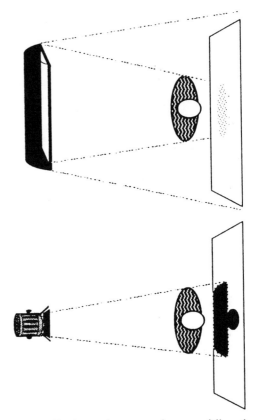

FIGURE 6.1 The larger the source, the more diffuse the light and the less dense the shadow.

CONTROLLING LIGHT QUALITY

Lighting units are generally selected for their ability to create or eliminate shadows, depending on their intended use. Sometimes it is preferable to illuminate a subject with completely shadowless lighting. This may be the case when shadows may interfere with an already intricate pattern, when shadows detract from the primary subject, or when soft, shadowless illumination suits the mood of the script. In these cases, it is wise to use the largest lighting units available.

37

In many lighting setups, hard sources of light are used to give shape, form, and character to the subjects. If a ball is illuminated with a completely shadowless light, it will photograph as a flat disk. When a hard spotlight is used, its round shape is immediately apparent. The shape of faces, bodies, and all other three-dimensional objects are revealed with clarity and vitality by directional luminaires.

Hard lights provide the directionality and characteristic look of the shot; soft lights raise the overall illumination levels and fill in dark shadows. The lighting quality of real settings can be duplicated by selecting instruments that cast the same type of shadows as the sources that illuminate the real settings.

THE LIGHTING FIXTURE

All artificial light sources must be installed in a fixture before they can be safely and conveniently used for lighting purposes. Most fixtures, also called *luminaires* or *instruments*, have a housing that is usually constructed of lightweight, heat-resistant sheet steel or aluminum. The housing pivots on a U-shaped yoke, which allows the fixture to be tilted and swiveled. The yoke is attached to a spud (or cylindrical pin) or C-clamp and is mounted on a light stand or hung from an overhead pipe.

LENSED FIXTURES

The lensed (or enclosed-type) fixture contains a condenser lens that is set in a cylindrical housing that completely surrounds the light source. Three brackets are attached to the housing in front of the lens to accept various accessories and filters. The box-shaped base of the housing contains the light socket and its reflector holder, both of which are attached to an external adjustment control. A power switch and cable complete the unit (see Figure 6.2).

Enclosed housings contain cooling slots to vent heat from the lamp in its upright position. On most fixtures, the internal lamp may be accessed through a hinged door on the front of the unit.

Reflector Design

Except for some carbon arc lamps, all enclosed fixtures use a reflector, which is usually a curved plate with a polished metallic surface. A reflector primarily redirects light, but some designs actually absorb infrared or UV radiation. Depending on the luminaire, the reflector may be spherical, ellipsoidal, parabolic, or a combination of these shapes. The shape of the reflector largely determines the *throw* (the effective length of its projected beam) and the quality of the light beam.

The spherical reflector is used in enclosed-type fixtures and scoops, the ellipsoidal reflector is used in both open-

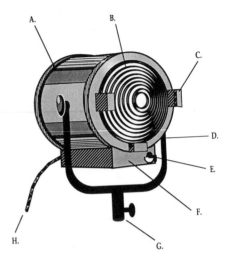

FIGURE 6.2 A typical lensed fixture incorporates cooling vents (A), a Fresnel lens (B), brackets for holding accessories (C), a yoke (D), a rudder for spotflood focus adjustments (E), an underbox (F) that contains a lamp and reflector mechanism, a receptacle for mounting on a stand or C-clamp (G), and a power cable (H).

faced and enclosed fixture types, and the parabolic design is found in sealed-beam lamps, such as the parabolic aluminized reflector (PAR). The combination reflector is used in the softlight.

The light socket and reflector are mounted together on rails and are linked mechanically to a focus adjustment knob. The knob (located on the front or rear base) is either of a semirotating paddle or rudder design, a rotating screw knob, or a sliding handle. The adjustment knob moves the socket and reflector toward the lens for floodlight position or away from the lens for spotlight applications.

Reflector design is crucial in indirect lighting fixtures, such as softlights, where all light emanates from the reflector, rather than from the globes themselves. Softlight reflectors may be large, troughlike units that emit scattered light over a wide area. Metallized umbrellas are often attached to various open-faced fixtures, essentially converting them into softlights.

Lens Design

Enclosed-type instruments used in motion picture and television production employ at least one plano-convex or Fresnel lens. Sealed-beam lamps use a self-contained, fluted lens design. Both designs refract the divergent rays of the radiating source and focus them in parallel or convergent beams.

The plano-convex lens, which has one flat surface and one convex surface, is the simplest design. Because of its great mass, it is quite heavy and does not dissipate heat. This lens is most often found in the ellipsoidal fixture.

The Fresnel lens was originally designed to replace the heavy plano-convex lens for use in lighthouses. The French

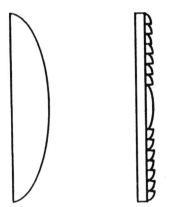

FIGURE 6.3 Plano-convex (left) and Fresnel lens (right) designs.

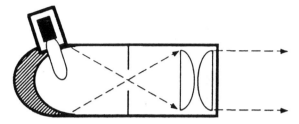

FIGURE 6.4 An ellipsoidal fixture generally includes an ellipsoidal reflector (A), internal shutters for shaping the light beam (B), and two plano-convex lenses (C).

physicist Augustine Jean Fresnel took the heavy, plano-convex lens, cut away most of its convex surface, and duplicated the curved contour with a recessed series of sloped concentric rings, which collect and direct radiant light into parallel beams (see Figure 6.3). The flat surface of the lens is also textured, which slightly diffuses the transmitted light. Light transmitted through the Fresnel falls off gradually enough to allow for two lamps to blend softly in adjacent areas.

The fluted lens, an integral part of PAR and other similar lamps, is discussed in "Sealed-Beam Lamps."

The Ellipsoidal Fixture

The ellipsoidal fixture, so called because of the shape of its reflector (see Figure 6.4), contains one or two plano-convex lenses, thereby giving the ellipsoidal fixture its characteristic long throw and ability to project a pattern on a given area. The ellipsoidal is sometimes called a *Leko light*.

The ellipsoidal housing contains four internal framing shutters, which can be adjusted to project a pool of light with hard, defined lines, such as a square or rectangle. The instrument's beam is focused by sliding the telescoping lens tube at the front of the fixture. Ellipsoidal fixtures, used primarily in theaters and sound stages, are somewhat heavy and unwieldy for location work. They do not have on/off switches and are usually mounted from overhead pipes or grids.

The Follow Spot

The follow spot, which may house several plano-convex or Fresnel lenses, is used when a concentrated, hard circle of light is needed to follow a moving performer. The larger models use a xenon, HMI, or carbon arc light source to achieve a 300-foot or 400-foot throw. The follow spot is usually mounted on a heavy stand.

All follow spots have a shutter, a reflector, a lens to focus the light, an on/off switch, a quick-focus handle, an iris, and a front housing (called a *boomerang*) that contains a set of filter holders. There is also a douser for complete beam blackout.

The color temperature of ellipsoidals and follow spots used in the theater may not be 3200°K. Therefore, it may be necessary to determine the color temperature of the fixtures and correct it by filtration. As a rule of thumb, arc follow spots are generally 5500°K and ellipsoidal fixtures are anywhere from 2800°K–3400°K.

The Fresnel Fixture

Because a Fresnel lens is relatively thin, lightweight, and efficient, it is the most common lens in use for film- and television-lighting fixtures. Luminaires that employ this type of lens are often simply called *Fresnels* and are designated by the wattage of the lamp they contain (e.g., 2K = 2000 watts, 5K = 5000 watts, etc.). A 10K Fresnel is sometimes called a *tener*, a 5K a *senior*, a 2K a *junior*, a 1K a *baby*, and a 650-watt is called a *tweenie*. A Fresnel fixture containing a lamp of fewer than 250 watts is known as an *inky-dink* or a *midget* and a Fresnel fixture less than 100 watts is called a *peewee*. Small Fresnels, which accommodate a 650-watt or lower wattage lamp, are also known as *peppers*.

A new Fresnel lamp, featuring an unpainted aluminum housing and a 12,000-watt HMI lamp, is called a *silver bullet* or *silver streak*.

SEALED-BEAM (PAR) LAMPS

The PAR lamp resembles an automobile headlight (see Figure 6.5); it has a tungsten filament, a silvered bowl reflector, and a fluted lens that is self-contained within the unit. The PAR angle of light is constant and may not be focused. To change the angle of light, the lamp must be changed for another lamp of a different beam shape. The PAR may be mounted inside a simple cylindrical housing called a *PAR can* or used in a module in clusters of up to 12 similar fixtures.

A *module* is a flat housing designed to accept a single PAR lamp. Modules are often combined in rows or clusters of two or three lamps and can be bracketed together to make up two-, four-, six-, nine-, or 12-lamp groupings. Clusters of this type are often used for outdoor applications as a substitute for carbon arc fixtures.

A rectangular housing fixture that incorporates two or

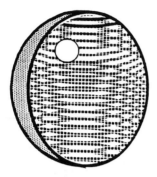

FIGURE 6.5 A parabolic aluminized reflector (PAR) lamp.

FIGURE 6.6 The Lowel Pro-light. (Courtesy Lowel-Light Mfg., Inc.)

three PARs and is mounted on top of a camera is called an *obie light*.

Advantages of the PAR can are its relatively low cost, light weight, and durability. The most widely used PAR can is designed to house the PAR 64—a 1000-watt, 3200°K lamp that is about 8 inches in diameter. Used extensively at rock concerts, its powerful punching beam with a soft edge has made the PAR 64 a favorite for lighting nighttime street scenes.

There are a variety of lamps available under the PAR designation. Each lamp is described by a three-letter code that specifies the beam width, wattage, and color temperature of each. One of the most common, the FAY lamp, is a 5000°K, 650-watt PAR globe with a dichroic filter built into the lens of the envelope.

OPEN-FACED FIXTURES

Enclosed fixtures, though versatile and controllable, are too heavy and bulky for some location work. Therefore, they are often augmented by fixtures that feature a lightweight, open-faced design.

Open-faced fixtures are those that have no lens; the light source is visible and easily accessible. Light rays are directed solely by the shape of the reflector. Open-faced fixtures are capable of much greater luminous intensity per watt than comparable enclosed fixtures, thereby making them ideal for location work. Some commonly used open-faced luminaires are the prime, compact, scoop, broad, softlight, and background fixtures.

Prime and Compact Fixtures

A *prime fixture* has a round housing, no base, and is fluted or perforated at the top to vent heat. Much of the intense heat generated by the lamp is dissipated at the open face of the instrument. Some prime fixtures have an on/off switch on the housing; most have an in-line switch on an AC cable that is connected directly to the housing. A focusing control at the back of the fixture controls the degree of flood or spot. Unlike the enclosed housing fixture, in which reflector and lamp move in conjunction, the light source is moved in relation to the reflector, which remains stationary.

The *compact fixture* is a small, portable prime fixture that draws fewer than 1000 watts. The Lowel Pro-light, for example (see Figure 6.6), offers a variety of interchangeable reflectors and numerous accessories for the location filmmaker.

A 2K, open-faced fixture is often called a *mighty*, a 1K a *mickey*, a 650W a *teeny*, and a 600W a *teeny-weeny*. Several manufacturers offer prime and compact fixtures as part of a location kit, which is an easily transportable case that contains three or four instruments, stands, and accessories.

Scoop and Broad Fixtures

Scoops and broads (see Figure 6.7) are used for soft fill light. The *scoop*, which is primarily a studio fixture, is so named for its large, bowl-shaped reflector, which also serves as the housing. The scoop produces an excellent, soft light over a widespread area. However, the scoop fixture is used infrequently on location, because it is heavy and cumbersome, and its light is difficult to control.

The *broad* consists of a tubular quartz bulb and a shallow, metal reflector set in a small, rectangular housing.

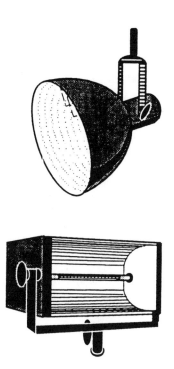

FIGURE 6.7 A scoop fixture (top) and a broad fixture (bottom).

FIGURE 6.8 The Lowel Tota-light. (Courtesy Lowel-Light Mfg., Inc.)

Single broad fixtures are not usually focusable, but multibulb units are focused often. The illumination produced by a broad fixture is spread over a wide area, but the light is not very diffused. Shadows can be as harsh as any as those produced by a spotlight. The broad fixture is particularly good for lighting an entire wall or other interior background. Because they are often tucked away in corners and other tight places on a shoot, small broad fixtures are frequently called *nook lights*. The broad tends to have a shorter throw than the scoop.

A popular and versatile variation on the broad is the Lowel Tota-light (see Figure 6.8), which can function as an indirect light with an attachable umbrella reflector.

Softlight Fixtures

The softlight (see Figure 6.9) is designed to direct illumination from the light source, which is shielded, into a large reflector that directs a soft spread of indirect light to the subject. The softlight has a rectangular, open face; a large reflector of either aluminum, baked white enamel, or metallized black cloth (as the Lowel Softlite); and, often, a double light source (usually two 1000-watt bulbs).

The illumination of a softlight is considerably more diffuse than that of a scoop and is so scattered that it appears to wrap around a subject, thus giving the impression of a shadowless illumination. The softlight, however, is a relatively inefficient instrument in terms of luminous intensity.

FIGURE 6.9 Softlight.

There are also softlights that incorporate a bank of four to eight fluorescent tubes, rather than tungsten lamps. These fixtures are useful as supplemental illumination on locations that are illuminated predominantly by overhead fluorescent panels. These softlights do not emit a great deal of light, but they balance well with the existing fluorescent light without needing filtration.

Background Fixtures

Background fixtures are used to evenly illuminate large background areas and include the pan and the strip light.

The *pan light* is a large-diameter, round-reflector fixture (see Figure 6.10) used for lighting scenery outside a window or door on a set. When used with diffusion sheets, it makes an excellent fill light as well.

Strip lights (or *cyc strips*) (see Figure 6.11) are multiple source units used along the tops and bottoms of backgrounds to provide wide illumination over broad surfaces, such as cycloramas and sky backdrops. They are usually run from dimmers (a rheostat that varies the amount of voltage flowing to a fixture or fixtures) and therefore have no on/off switch.

Dimmers were used extensively in the days of black-and-white photography as a means of decreasing and increasing illumination. Because reducing voltage to a tungsten source adversely lowers its color temperature, dimmers have fallen from favor with the universal adoption of color film stock. Dimmers are sometimes used when its light-warming effects are desired. A light control panel in a studio or stage is often referred to as a *dimmer*, whether it uses rheostats or not.

SAFETY PRECAUTIONS

Since lighting instruments are heavy, cumbersome, and draw great amounts of electrical power, they present potential hazards if they are not treated with special care.

Always anchor the base of a light stand, Century stand (C-stand), or reflector stand with a suitable-size sandbag in order to keep the fixture from toppling. Special red canvas sandbags with built-in carrying straps are available in 15- and 35-pound weights for this purpose. It is particularly important to anchor all lightweight aluminum stands and

any stand extended to its full height. A good rule of thumb is to use one sandbag for every rise of the stand you extend. Many gaffers route the fixture's AC cable through a round, keyring-type clip attached to the base of the stand. Finally, all cables should be taped down securely to the floor or walls with gaffer tape.

Make sure that all fixtures are mounted right side up, with the cooling louvers on top. A fixture should never be allowed to operate in an inverted position, which defeats the venting design and shortens the life of the lamp.

LIGHTING ACCESSORIES

Next to the fixtures themselves, lighting accessories are the most important tools used to control illumination. They provide the means to change and manipulate light beam shape, intensity, quality, and color temperature. Lighting accessories may be classified according to the way each is employed, whether they affix to the instrument or light stand, whether they are separately mounted go-betweens called *gobos*, whether they are peripheral accessories, such as sandbags and apple boxes, and whether they are durable or expendable items.

Fixture-Mounted Accessories

Barndoors
A barndoor (see Figure 6.12) resembles a kind of bonnet that attaches to the front of a fixture; it has two or four adjustable, hinged, black metal blades or "doors." The barndoor has a flange or bracket that enables it to slide into a holder on the front of a fixture. Some barndoors may be rotated in the holder; other barndoors are fixed.

FIGURE 6.10 A pan fixture.

FIGURE 6.11 A striplight.

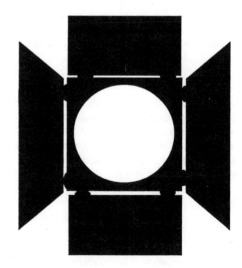

FIGURE 6.12 Barndoors.

A barndoor is used to keep extraneous light from falling on given areas of a set and it controls light by creating a soft-edged transition between lighted and shaded areas. The blades may be adjusted in any position between fully closed and fully open. The doors are often brought together to form a slit of light so that a sign or other detail can be highlighted. Barndoors, while effective on directional light fixtures, do little to control the highly diffused illumination of softlights. For this situation, a gridlike, bladed accessory called an *eggcrate* may be placed on the indirect lighting fixture to keep the beam tighter. An eggcrate looks like a Christmas ornament box with the bottom removed (see Figure 6.13).

Scrims

Scrims are the primary tools for dimming a light beam without adversely affecting its color temperature. Scrims are circular metal screens that fit into the same front brackets of a lighting fixture that hold the barndoor. The screen, which comes in various thicknesses, covers any portion or all of the scrim; it is usually made of stainless steel to withstand the intense heat given off by the fixture. The most common are one-quarter, one-half, and full scrims (see Figure 6.14). Scrims also come in single- or double-mesh densities. The scrim cuts the intensity of a beam without greatly diffusing it. Fabric scrims, which mount on separate stands, are called *nets*.

Snoots

A snoot is a conical or cylindrical piece that attaches to the front of a fixture (see Figure 6.15) to concentrate the beam into a small, round area and eliminate spill light. Snoots are used to highlight and isolate selected areas in a scene, such as a single table in a nightclub. When a snoot is not available, one may be improvised with a heavy flat black foil known as *black wrap*.

Goosenecks

A gooseneck is a flexible tube that attaches with a clamp to the yoke of an instrument and holds a small gobo in the light beam to take down a flare or to eliminate a highlight.

Gobos

A *gobo* is a generic term for any opaque unit used to eliminate light from a particular area in a scene. Gobos are usually mounted on C-stands or gobo stands (see Figure 6.16). A gobo head is fitted to a C-stand and accepts gobo rod extension arms of various diameters that can be rotated in any position. Many C-stands have a sliding leg that adjusts to level the stand on an uneven surface; this is called a *Rocky Mountain leg*.

Flags

The most common gobo is the *flag*—a rectangular wire frame covered with duvetyne, which is a black fabric. A flag is used to block an area from light emanating from a fixture. Flags

FIGURE 6.13 An eggcrate.

FIGURE 6.14 Scrims.

FIGURE 6.15 A snoot.

vary in size from 12 × 18in up to 30 ×36in. A *cutter* is a long narrow flag used when light from more than one side-by-side fixture is to be controlled or when the shadow of a microphone boom must be eliminated. A *blade* is a small narrow flag, frequently made of translucent acrylic. *Targets* and *dots* are circular flags that can be introduced into a light beam to shade small areas, particularly useful for toning down harsh highlights and other hot spots (see Figure 6.17).

Nets and Silks

The terms *scrim* and *net* are often used interchangeably to describe woven screen materials that reduce the amount of

FIGURE 6.16 C-stand with double arm head assembly holding a flag.

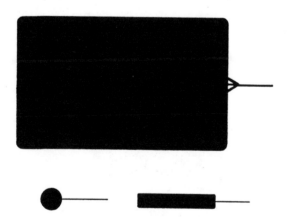

FIGURE 6.17 Flag, dot, and blade.

light falling on a subject. In general, a scrim is made of metal and a net is made of cloth.

A net is made of cloth-mesh material stretched on a frame (see Figure 6.18) and mounted on a C-stand. A cloth net may be used close to a Fresnel instrument when it is in the full flood position, but should not be placed too close when the lamp is spotted down, as the heat will damage the fabric. A net should never be placed close to an open-faced fixture.

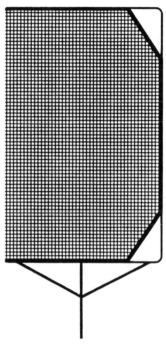

FIGURE 6.18 A net. The feathered edge creates smooth blends between light and dark areas.

A hexagonal weave (a honeycomb pattern) net fabric is preferred for professional lighting, as, unlike the traditional screendoor-type weaves, a hexagonal weave breaks up light most evenly. Of course, the more threads (and fewer openings) in a weave, the less light will pass through.

Black nets tend to cut light intensity with a minimum diffusion effect, lavender nets add diffusion, and white nets soften the light considerably. Nets come in several "strengths," depending on how many layers of weave are used. A net with a single layer that is color-coded green cuts about 30% of the passing light, while a double red net cuts transmitted light by 50%. A single lavender net cuts light by 15%.

A *silk* is a white, fine-weaved net used primarily for adding diffusion. The amount of light the silk passes depends on the proximity of the silk to the light source. When sandwiching two or more nets, a moire pattern (a plaid effect) can be eliminated by rotating one of the nets in relation to the other.

Miniature nets are available in various shapes and sizes, and are often used in flexible goosenecks to reduce light that is falling in specific areas within an otherwise evenly lighted area. In practice, the key light (or lights) is usually set first, each area of the set is given the proper illumination, and any obvious double shadows are eliminated. Large softlights are then placed near the camera, if possible, so that any shadows they create will fall behind the subject. The amount of fill light is adjusted to bring the shadows to the desirable exposure range. This lighting ratio is expressed as 2:1, 3:1, 4:1, and so forth. A 2:1 ratio means that the fill light is one half as bright as the key light—a difference of one f-stop.

Butterflies

A *butterfly* is a large net (measuring 4ft × 4ft or larger) used to reduce the sunlight falling on a subject and is supported by a single stand. The butterfly is big enough to cover a medium shot or two-shot and reduces the harsh look of hard sunlight (see Figure 6.19). When a translucent material is used on a butterfly frame, it is called a *silk*. When a butterfly frame is stretched with black duvetyne, it becomes a solid (really a giant flag). In order to maintain shade in changing sunlight, using a solid is often a wise alternative to re-setting up a shot.

Butterflies are often set at an angle, rather than being held in a horizontal position. Butterflies and overheads often come as kits, including stands, sectional frame, single and double nets, silks, and a solid.

Overheads

An *overhead* is a very large frame that measures up to 20-foot square and supports a stretched net, silk, or solid (a large flag). An overhead is used to filter or block light from a two-shot or three-shot and also to shade any large prop, such as an automobile. The overhead is supported by two heavy roller stands with oversized gobo heads. Overhead stands, used to hold anything that has to extend higher than the reach of a C-stand are often called *high rollers*. Wind can wreak havoc with a large overhead, hence they are often secured to the ground with ropes.

Cookies and Frames

A *cookie* (or *cukaloris*) is a sheet of plywood, painted screen, or other material perforated with irregular holes (see Figure 6.20). When placed in front of a light source, the cukaloris breaks up the beam and projects a mottled pattern of light and shadow. The effect is useful for eliminating glare from reflective flat surfaces and adding visual interest to walls and backgrounds. The cast pattern becomes more distinct as the cukaloris is moved away from the light source and closer to the subject. A *frame* is a plywood cukaloris cut to project patterns of venetian blinds, paned windows, prison bars, or any other silhouette across a set.

Reflectors

Reflectors (which include heavy, stand-mounted shiny boards and lightweight reflectors such as flexfills, foam core, and reflective polyester sheets) are essential for daytime lighting in most exterior locations. They are often used exclusively in place of exterior lighting instruments.

Shiny Boards

A *shiny board* (or reflector board) is a large, rigid panel that pivots on a yoke that is mounted on a heavy stand (see Figure 6.21). The shiny board has two metallic sides—one "hard" and one "soft." The hard side of the shiny board is a smooth reflective surface that reflects a highly specular light. The soft side bears a gridwork of delicate foil leafing that breaks up the light to provide a softer light. These silvered surfaces are used to bounce the sun's rays into shaded areas to reduce the contrast between sunlight and shadow.

Shiny boards are usually surfaced with silver-colored foil, but other colors are also available. A gold surface reflects an amber light and can imitate sunset or sunrise effects. Gold reflectors give a pleasing warmth to flesh tones and particularly enhance the appearance of dark-complected actors.

FIGURE 6.19 Butterfly.

FIGURE 6.20 A cukaloris (or cookie).

FIGURE 6.21 Shiny board (diffused side).

They also impart a lush, saturated look to plants and foliage in general. Blue- or cool-surfaced reflectors are sometimes used to boost the color temperature of a reflected tungsten lamp or the setting sun to 5500°K.

A board can be used as a key light, fill light, or a kicker (to back light a subject). If the light is too intense, a slip-on net may be used to cut down the intensity of the light. These slip-on nets should only be used on the hard side of the board, for they will wear away the foil leaf grid if used over the soft side.

A shiny board must be positioned properly in relation to the sun to catch its rays. The easiest way to aim the reflector is to point the reflector at the sun, tilt the reflector down until the reflected beam can be seen on the ground, swivel the board until the beam is just under the subject, and tilt the board up until the reflected beam illuminates the subject.

Under gusty conditions, shiny boards may be difficult to control and should be attended by a grip (an assistant) at all times. In general, be careful not to aim the reflector so that

the actors are forced to squint; instead, move it off to one side of the camera to keep glare from the actor's line of sight. The reflector should also reflect light on the subject from above eye level if a natural effect is desired. Don't let the board wobble in the wind so that the light shimmers on the actor's face. Lock the reflector board down and secure it firmly with sandbags. If the reflector light is too harsh, move the unit back or place a net over the board. When the shot is completed, the board should be tipped so that it is parallel to the ground with minimum surface to the wind.

Shiny boards have some disadvantages. Changing weather can create costly delays as clouds pass over the sun. In any case, the board will need to be constantly adjusted as the earth's rotation changes the relative angle of the sun to the reflector. The flat, broad reflector boards catch the wind as well as the sun, and may tip over if they are not secured with sandbags or individually manned. Stands can often telescope to a height of 10 feet or more, but extended high-rise stands can be particularly hard to control. Shiny boards are heavy and rigid, and may require a pickup truck to transport them.

Lightweight Reflectors   The general unwieldiness of conventional reflector boards has encouraged the use of lighter, less cumbersome units on small-scale shoots.

Durable, metallized polyester (mylar) sheets, available in many different colors and textures, can be shaped and configured in various ways. They can be used in automobile interiors to reflect light onto faces and are also very handy for shooting in very small rooms, booths, passageways, and any number of other tight places.

Flexfills, which resemble large drum heads with one shiny side and one white side, are made of fabric that is stretched on collapsible frames. They are light and compact, but must be held steady by a grip.

Foam core, a stiff, Styrofoam-center construction board available in 32 × 40-inch and 40 × 60-inch sheets, is a very popular reflector. Foam core has two brilliant white surfaces (one of which can be metallized by applying aluminum foil) and is also available with silver and gold metallic surfaces. All lightweight reflectors are susceptible to wobbling in the slightest air turbulence, so be very careful when using them outdoors or in drafty interiors.

Bead board is another popular reflector material. It is a fibrous, porous sheet that can also serve as a sound-dampening panel as well as a bounce lighting board.

Other Accessories

There is a wide array of other standard and improvised accessories used in film and video lighting. Some of the more common are discussed on the following pages.

An *apple box* (see Figure 6.22) is a closed wooden box with a grip hole on each side of the box. The apple box, which comes in several sizes, is used for propping up stands and raising equipment or actors to a higher elevation.

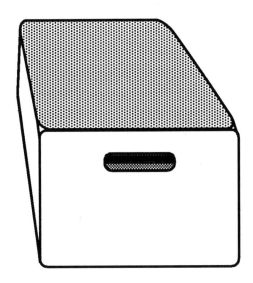

FIGURE 6.22 Apple box.

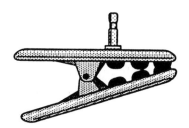

FIGURE 6.23 Gaffer (gator) grip.

A *cup block* looks like a wooden ashtray mold with a shallow, bowllike recess and is used to stabilize wheeled stands and prevent them from rolling away.

A *flex arm* is an articulated extension arm with a number of ball joints designed to hold small gobos, such as dots. With a clamp at one end and a ¼-inch diameter locking receiver at the other, the flex arm is affixed to a C-stand (unlike the gooseneck, which mounts to the fixture itself). The gobo at the opposite end is placed across the light beam to cut down a flare or eliminate a highlight.

The *gaffer grip* (or *gator grip*) is a giant alligator clip with one or two ⅝-inch pins on the handle and/or jaws (see Figure 6.23). The gaffer grip is used to mount lightweight fixtures to doors, chairs, tables, pipes, and other places that may offer a stable grip. It is also handy for securing foam core sheets.

Grip clips look like big metal clothespins, but are not as heavy as gaffer grips, and are available in four sizes. Grip clips have a variety of uses—to fasten gels, foam core boards, and other lightweight articles to stands and fixtures.

Pole cats are adjustable poles that extend vertically or horizontally between floor and ceiling or between two walls to hold lightweight fixtures.

Expendables

Any accessories that are used up or expended over a period of time are called *expendables*. Expendables include diffusion material, colored gels, and tape.

Diffusion is a term to describe any material that breaks up and scatters the light beam so that it appears to be larger and softer (i.e., shadows are less distinct or practically nonexistent) than its original source.

A diffused light source is difficult to control with barndoors and flags, due to the scatter of its light rays. The degree to which diffusion material reduces and softens light depends upon the density of the material used.

Silk is a term for any cloth material that has a bright translucence. Tafetta, an artificial fabric, is finding greater use in "silks," as it is more durable than traditional China silk. Heavier diffusion cloth of cotton or nylon is called *gauze*. Photographers have often been known to use white bedsheets as diffusion gauze. Any diffusion material made of cloth must be placed away from light sources for obvious reasons.

Frosted gelatin, a highly fragile material once used widely for diffusion purposes, has been phased out in favor of the more durable plastics. *Acetate* is a stiff, sheet material that should be mounted on a C-stand in front of a fixture. If acetate is placed on the fixture, the heat will cause it to warp and melt. *Polyester sheeting* has become very popular because of its high durability. *Spun glass* is also popular as a diffusion material. Although it will not burn, spun glass may darken when placed too close to a fixture; another disadvantage is its skin-irritating fibers.

Filter gels are widely available in many colors and include color-balancing filters, color-compensating filters, and special color effects filters.

Diffusion and colored acrylic sheets, more durable than gels, are also readily available.

It is advisable to test the light transmission factor of any gel before using it in a shoot. This may be accomplished simply by taking an incident light meter reading (see Chapter Seven) of a given source and comparing it to a reading of the same light through the material in question.

Other commonly used expendables include *gaffer tape*, a strong, fiber-backed, all-purpose adhesive tape used to fasten down cables and provide temporary joints. While similar to the often substituted and cheaper duct tape, gaffer tape offers greater bonding properties, is easily removable, and tends to leave less residue than the cheaper tape. Be aware that gaffer tape will pull up paint from any finished surface to which it is applied.

Wooden, spring-type clothespins, colloquially called *C-47s*, are often used to affix diffusion and colored media to barndoors and frames. Other expendables include *dulling spray*, which is an aerosol sprayed on glossy surfaces to take down glare, and *smoke liquid* for fog machines.

A widely used expendable material is *foam core*, a stiff, Styrofoam-center construction board often used as a reflector. A *show card* is another stiff art board used for bounce lighting; it comes in sizes as large as 48-in by 60-in and has a matte black surface on one side, in addition to one white surface. The black side makes the show card useful as a flag.

Another popular, expendable reflector material is *Griffolyn*, the trade name for an extremely durable, three-ply rubber sheeting. Griffolyn sheets come in 6 × 6-foot, 12 × 12-foot, and 20 × 20-foot sizes, and are usually stretched on frames and mounted on heavy stands. Foam core, show cards, and Griffolyn (all lightweight materials) are susceptible to fluttering in the slightest air turbulence, so be very careful when using them in breezy or drafty conditions.

Self-Study

■ QUESTIONS

1. The plano-convex lens is most often used in the _____ fixture.
   a. PAR
   b. ellipsoidal
   c. Fresnel

2. You must have the correct size _____ in order to fasten a fixture safely to a light stand.
   a. yoke
   b. spud
   c. blimp

3. The _____ was originally developed for use in lighthouses.
   a. Fresnel
   b. PAR
   c. broad

4. The term *baby* refers to _____.
   a. a 200-watt, open-faced fixture
   b. a 225-amp arc lamp
   c. a 1000-watt Fresnel fixture

5. A PAR lamp with a special, dichroic lens is called a _____.
   a. junior
   b. half-gallon
   c. FAY

6. A paddle or rudder on a fixture _____.
   a. is affixed to the front to shape the light beam
   b. is used to focus the light
   c. is used with a spud to mount the fixture

7. An accessory that can be attached directly to a fixture to cut intensity without affecting the quality of the beam is called a _____.
   a. scrim
   b. net
   c. silk

8. The best fixture to use to create a hard-edged, disk-shaped pool of light is the _____.
   a. Fresnel
   b. scoop
   c. ellipsoidal

9. The family of gobos known as flags does not include _____.
   a. cutters
   b. dots
   c. rudders

10. The best accessory to use in front of a lamp to create interesting patterns on a wall is the _____
   a. snoot
   b. cukaloris
   c. net

■ ANSWERS

1. b. The plano-convex lens, which has one flat and one convex surface, is a standard component of the ellipsoidal fixture. Because of their weight, plano-convex lenses are used infrequently in film and video lighting instruments. The PAR uses a fluted lens and the Fresnel fixture uses the familiar, concentric circle ridge design.

2. b. The spud is the cylindrical piece that fits into a receptacle on the stand and is used to secure a fixture to a light stand. A spud must be of correct diameter to function safely. The size of the yoke has nothing to do with the mounting of the fixture and a blimp is an accessory used to deaden sound emanating from a motion picture camera.

3. a. The Fresnel lens was designed specifically for use in lighthouses by the French physicist Augustine Jean Fresnel. The PAR was originally designed to be used in sealed-beam headlamps. A broad is a specific, open-faced location fixture.

4. c. A *baby* is a 1K Fresnel spotlight. A *midget* is a 250- or 200-watt Fresnel fixture, while a *brute* is a 225-amp arc lamp.

5. c. A FAY is a PAR that contains dichroic filters that provide 5000°K of light. A 1000-watt soft lamp is sometimes called a *half-gallon* and a *junior* is a 2K Fresnel fixture.

6. b. A paddle or rudder is a spot-flood control on a fixture used to focus the light.

7. a. A scrim is a metal screen designed to fit directly on the front of a fixture; it cuts the intensity of the light without diffusing it appreciably. A net is too large, bulky, and flammable to attach directly to a fixture; it must be mounted on a C-stand several feet away from the lighting instrument. A silk is used as diffusion material and must be mounted on a C-stand.

8. c. The ellipsoidal fixture has a projectorlike ability to focus a hard beam, thanks to its adjustable, plano-convex lenses. A Fresnel, though a directional, focusable fixture, is incapable of casting a beam with a true hard edge. The scoop is a nonfocusing, open-faced, soft light source.

9. c. The rudder, a built-in lever used to focus a fixture, is not a gobo. A cutter is a long flag and dots are small, disk-shaped flags used to eliminate hot spots.

10. b. The cukaloris (or cookie) will create an interesting mottled or variegated pattern when a beam of light is cast through it. A snoot will shape and direct light into a tight circular pool, but will not create other patterns. A net will reduce the intensity of a source without otherwise affecting the quality of its light.

■ PROJECT 6.1:   QUALITIES OF VARIOUS FIXTURES AND ACCESSORIES

Purpose:

To vary light quality in one-source lighting situations.

Materials Needed:

model
video camcorder or camera and VCR
tripod
table lamp or candle
open-faced compact fixture with barndoors and stand (a Lowel Pro-light, Omni-light, or Mole-Richardson teenie or
   mickey will do nicely) or a broad fixture with a light stand (such as a Mole Nooklight or Lowel Tota-light)

one softlight with light stand (or compact or broad fixture used in conjunction with an umbrella or foam core panel)
one C-stand
one lavender, silk, toughspun, or any diffusion sheet, such as gauze, a sheet, or a plastic shower curtain liner
two sandbags
two grounded, AC extension cables
one 30 × 40-inch foam core sheet
black wrap
cukaloris (optional)
accessories as needed (gaffer tape, gels, clothespins, etc.)

Procedure:

The beauty of one-source lighting is its simplicity; it can be achieved with an open window or a single candle. The purpose here, however, is to experiment with as many different fixtures and accessories as possible, so long as you only use one actual light source at a time.

NOTE: Use whatever resources you have available. If you do not have any compact fixtures, you might use photofloods or even household bulbs mounted in bell-type utility scoops. If you do not have PAR cans, use an outdoor-type flood lamp. You can purchase a servicable, tungsten-halogen broad fixture (although it might not be 3200°K) for less than $20 at any do-it-yourself store. Black wrap can make fine snoots, flags, and cookies, while diffusion materials can be fashioned from anything translucent—from shower curtain linings to white bedsheets. So use your imagination (you will, anyway, as you design more intricate lighting plans).

1. Set up the video camera and recorder, and tape each of the following setups: Pose your model in a comfortable position (whether seated, standing, or reclining) about 4 feet from a side wall. Place your light source at eye level, on the opposite side and 90° from the subject. This positioning will create a crosslight that will leave half your subject in shadow. This crosslight makes it easy to judge the quality of the different sources you will be using. Look for the transition between highlight and shadow on the subject's face with each type of lighting instrument used, and note whether the gradation is abrupt or subtle. Also notice the kind of shadow cast in each setup—the shadow always indicates the quality (and direction) of the lighting.
2. Set up a table lamp (with its shade removed) or a candle to illuminate the subject. This setup is an example of a radiating source. Repeat this procedure in each of the following steps using

   a compact fixture with barndoors in spot mode, in flood position, and in flood mode with diffusion (this can be toughspun that is pinned to the barndoors using clothespins, a silk mounted on a C-stand head, or diffusion material hung from a C-stand gobo arm)
   a lensed source, such as a Fresnal (in spotlight mode) or PAR. Set up a cookie (you can fashion one from black wrap or a card if a commercially made cookie is not available) in front of the source
   soft light
   bounce lighting, only, from a card

Evaluating the Results:

Notice how one-source lighting can be the most natural illumination, since we often encounter these situations everyday. In general, it is best to use as few lighting sources as possible for any situation. One-source lighting is aesthetically desirable, because it usually appears to be justified and logical; it creates only one set of shadows. Bouncing light off a white wall, ceiling, or reflectors is often all that is required to augment the source and to fill in a dark shadow. Film and video are used to record subjects in motion and often several subjects at once. Therefore, despite the natural beauty of one-source lighting, film and video usually require the use of several light sources. This requires a knowledge and control of light direction and balance.

CHAPTER SEVEN

Measuring Light Intensity

INTRODUCTION

The cinematographer must consider light in five different ways—how much (intensity), what kind (quality), what color (color temperature), how it falls (direction), and how many sources (balance). The most basic skill in cinematography involves measuring and controlling the quantity or amount of light reaching the film.

PHOTOMETRY

The science of light measurement is called *photometry*. The standard unit for light measurement was originally based on the visible radiation of a single candle, called the *standard candle*. The old standard candle has been superseded by the *candela*, which is defined as 1/60th of the luminous intensity of a black body that has the temperature at which platinum melts.

It is important to distinguish between and among terms that refer to the light source itself, the amount of light falling on a given surface, and the brightness of the light reflected from the illuminated surface.

The illumination emitted from a light source is called *luminous intensity* and is measured in candelas or candles. The sum total of light falling on a subject is known as *incident light*. Subjects that are illuminated reflect some of the incident light; this is known as *reflected light.*

Luminous intensity and illumination are terms that refer to systems for measuring incident light, while reflected light is measured in terms of luminance. *Brightness* is a general term that is often used interchangeably with illumination and luminance.

In the United States, luminous intensity is most commonly measured in *footcandles*. The footcandle is the amount of incident light measured at a point that is 1 foot from a candela. The *lux* is the international metric counterpart to the footcandle (1 footcandle = 10.76 lux). The light sensitivity of video camera pickup tubes is often calibrated in lux (see Figure 7.1).

INCIDENT LIGHT

The total footcandles of illumination falling on a given surface depends on

the luminous intensity of the source

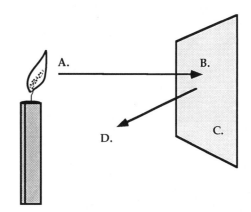

FIGURE 7.1 Photometric terms. *Luminous intensity* (A), measured in candelas, is the amount of light emitted from a source. The sum total of all light falling on a subject is called *incident light* (B). In the United States, the measure of incident light is the footcandle (everyone else uses lux). The amount of illumination striking an area that is 1 square foot at a 1-foot distance equals 1 lumen (C). Light emanating from a reflective surface is known as *luminance* or *reflected light* (D), which is measured in footlamberts.

the efficiency of the optical system used (in the case of a lamp)

the distance between the source and the surface

the absorption of the medium through which the light travels (air, haze, water, smoke, filters, etc.)

Lumens and Watts

Light sources are commonly rated in terms of their *wattage*. The wattage of a lamp describes the amount of power the source consumes, but corresponds only roughly to the amount of light produced. For instance, fluorescent and discharge sources deliver more light per watt than incandescent lamps. A more accurate measurement of actual light produced by a source is the *lumen*. One footcandle is equal to the illumination of an area that is 1 foot from a candle light source. The lumen is equal to a 1-foot square portion of this sphere. One candela produces one footcandle (or 12.57 lumens).

The Inverse Square Law

Rays of light emitted from a point source tend to spread farther and farther apart as they travel away from the source. The farther the light travels, the less the rays are able to illuminate a given object. This divergence of light rays, which results in a progressively weaker light over an increasing distance, is called *falloff*.

The amount of falloff in a given situation may be computed by a simple formula. When the distance from a light source to a given subject changes, the illumination is increased or reduced by the square of that amount. This is called the *inverse square law* and it states that the intensity of illumination at a given surface is inversely proportionate to the square of the distance between the source and the surface (see Figure 7.2). The inverse square law may be expressed as an equation:

$$\text{intensity} = \frac{1}{\text{distance squared}}$$

If a subject that is 5 feet from a light source receiving 400 footcandles of light intensity is moved 10 feet away, the surface will receive only one-quarter of the original illumination, or 100 footcandles. If the subject is moved 5 feet farther from the source, a total distance of 15 feet, the subject will receive one-ninth the original illumination, or just more than 44 footcandles. The same thing happens in reverse when the distance between a source and a subject is reduced. Thus, a subject illuminated with 20 footcandles at 20 feet would receive 80 footcandles at 10 feet.

The inverse square law is only strictly true for the uniformly diverging rays from a point source that have not been modified by a lens or reflector. Nonetheless, it is an underlying principle in solving many lighting problems.

REFLECTED LIGHT

To measure light reflected from a surface (luminance), four factors must be considered:

the incident light
the value of the surface, whether light or dark (reflectance)
the texture of the surface, whether matte or shiny
the angle at which the measurement is taken, especially when
    measuring specular surfaces

THE EXPOSURE METER

We have seen that there are two ways to measure quantities of light—the amount of light falling on a subject (incident light) and the amount of light reflected from a subject (reflected light). The cinematographer measures light according to one of these two systems using an exposure meter designed to measure incident light, reflected light, or both.

Most modern exposure meters may be classified as either *photovoltaic* or *photoconductive*. The photovoltaic meter uses a light-sensitive cell consisting of selenium that is bonded to a metal base plate and covered with a thin film of gold or platinum. As light falls on the cell, current is gener-

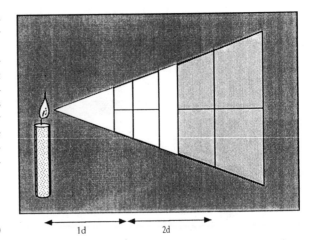

FIGURE 7.2 The inverse square law states that light intensity is inversely proportionate to the distance between the source and the illuminated surface, squared. Hence, the light illuminating a surface at 1 foot spreads out at 2 feet away to cover an area four times as large.

ated and measured by a microammeter, which measures minute amounts of voltage.

As a greater amount of light falls on the cell, more current is generated and a higher reading is displayed on the meter, and vice versa. Meters of this type are simple in construction and require very little maintenance. The cells have a spectral sensitivity similar to film emulsions, so no special color compensation is necessary.

The one drawback to the selenium, photovoltaic meter is its relatively poor sensitivity to low light levels. Nevertheless, the rugged, selenium meter design is well suited for incident-type meters used in the motion picture industry. If there is not enough light to move the needle on the light meter, there usually isn't enough light to shoot the film. However, for situations involving high-speed film and low light levels, and for reflected, spot, and through-the-lens (TTL) applications, a different meter design is often used.

The photoconductive meter uses a cell made of cadmium sulfide (CdS). Unlike the selenium cell, which produces a minute voltage when struck by light, the CdS cell acts as a semiconductor that varies its electrical resistance according to the amount of light that strikes it. A battery provides the current and the CdS regulates the amount of that current by its variable resistance. The changes in current are then displayed by the microammeter as a light reading.

The advantage of the CdS cell is its high sensitivity—about ten times that of an equivalent selenium meter. This feature makes the CdS cell well suited for very low-light situations. For this reason, CdS cells are used almost exclusively in reflected light meters, especially spot meters and TTL metering systems.

Light meters incorporating CdS cells are very versatile and are often sensitive enough to give readings in moonlight.

There are, however, definite disadvantages. For one, they use batteries and, like so many battery-powered instruments, frequently need re-calibration due to voltage inconsistencies when batteries inevitably run down. Batteries and the voltage-regulating circuits that often accompany them add extra weight and bulk to the meter as well. The CdS cell also suffers from sensitivity lag—a problem similar to light lag exhibited by certain video pickup tubes in low-light situations. In dim light, the meter does not respond very quickly to small changes in illumination.

LIGHT METER DESIGNS

Modern light meter designs fall into four categories, with some models able to convert from one type to another (when accompanied by accessories):

hand-held, reflected light meters
reflected light spot meters
through-the-lens reflected light meters
incident light meters

Reflected Light Meters

Reflected light meters are designed with the light-sensitive cell located behind some sort of shield to control the light acceptance angle. This shield may be a perforated grid, a simple narrow tube, or a lenticular magnifier. The purpose of the design is to produce a meter that is more or less directional, so that the meter can be pointed toward a given object and not read light from all directions at once.

The reflected meter, which reads the brightness of the light reflected by objects in the scene, is calibrated for 18% reflectance (medium gray). Cinematographers must decide whether they want the subject to be reproduced as medium gray. For instance, a light-colored face reflects about 36% light, while a dark-colored face may have less than 18% reflectance. The meter, however, reads each face as having 18% reflectance and will not give ideal readings, thereby underexposing light flesh tones and overexposing the darker complexions. The way to avoid guesswork is to use an 18% reflectance gray card and measure the light reflecting off of it, instead of off of the subject.

There are several ways to use a reflected meter—taking integrated readings of a complete scene, measuring specific tonal areas, and reading an 18% reflective gray card.

An integrated reading of a complete scene is the most common method of using the reflected light meter, particularly among amateurs. This is also the least accurate method. Depending on how the meter is aimed at the scene, it may take in too much bright sky or dark earth and thus give false readings.

Measuring specific tonal areas of the scene will lead to more accurate exposure control. Reflected light readings of the darkest and lightest areas are taken and an exposure value is chosen from these two extremes. Such an exposure should, as closely as possible, capture the entire tonal range.

The third technique is to use the reflected light meter to read a subject of known and constant reflectance, usually a gray card. The gray card is specially designed to reflect 18% of the light that strikes it, which is an average of the brightest, the darkest, and all the intermediate tones of any given scene. These medium-gray cards correspond to the calibration of incident meters and enable the reflected meter to give the same reading (when used properly) as an incident meter. The card should be angled halfway between the light source and the camera for the most accurate reading.

Spot Meters

Spot meters are reflected light meters fitted with a lens (see Figure 7.3) and allow only a very narrow angle of acceptance, usually from .5°–5°. Because the measuring angle is so small, spot meters also have a viewfinder. Spot meters are capable of giving accurate readings of small portions of a scene. They will also measure flesh tones from great distances, making them ideal to use with long camera lenses.

Spot meters are ideal in situations where taking incident light readings would be inconvenient or impossible, such as at a concert or similar event. Unfortunately, like most specialized precision instruments, they are very expensive.

Through-the-Lens Meters

TTL meters are, essentially, spot meters built into camera bodies. With the advent of reflex cameras and zoom lenses with reflex viewing systems, it was a natural step to place a tiny, light-sensitive cell in the reflex light path and thus constantly monitor the brightness of the scene as viewed by the camera. The TTL meter has evolved into the fully automatic exposure system wherein the CdS cell controls a current powering a tiny motor that instantly sets the aperture (or shutter speed).

There are two important drawbacks to the TTL metering system, due to its uncritical reliance on the basic reflected light meter. First, because this system essentially gives an integrated reflected light reading, it does not produce consistent flesh tones due to changes in backgrounds and objects

FIGURE 7.3 A spot meter.

surrounding the subject. Second, when a camera pans from a dark scene to a lighter one, the result is often a distracting and abrupt aperture change.

Incident Meters

Since the incident light meter is the most valuable and versatile meter for motion picture and video lighting, we will devote the greatest part of our discussion to it.

The *incident light meter* is always recognizable by its round, white plastic dome (*lumisphere* or *photosphere*), which acts as a three-dimensional, light-gathering surface. The light-sensitive cell is located behind the dome and senses the total intensity of the light striking the dome.

The incident meter is used to measure light falling on a scene and is usually held at the subject position with the dome aimed at the camera lens. The dome is designed to simulate the shape of a person's face or other three-dimensional object within a scene. The advantage of this design is that the dome will automatically give a balanced reading of one or more light sources striking the subject. Thus, readings are integrated in a way that corresponds to relative light and dark portions of the three-dimensional subjects within a scene. The incident meter is often used for determining exposure; however its most important feature is its usefulness in determining lighting ratios.

Using the Incident Meter

Popular incident meters include the Spectra Pro and the Sekonic Studio Deluxe. The American-made Spectra has its calculator dial on the back of the meter, while the Japanese-made Sekonic has a dial on its front side (see Figure 7.4). Despite their superficial differences, they work in the same basic ways. A meter that has recently gained widespread popularity is the Minolta Flash Meter IV, which features a microcomputer and liquid crystal display (LCD) digital readout. Originally designed for photographers who use electronic flash, this meter is extremely useful for cinematographers, due to its direct fps and motion picture shutter speed readings.

The readings given by most meters usually need to be interpreted in order to determine proper exposure; this is the purpose of the calculator dial mounted on the meter (see Figure 7.5). These calculators vary in design, but all have at least four dials that correspond to four variables—film sensitivity, exposure time, lens aperture, and scene brightness.

An exposure index dial is on each calculator. The IE dial has an indicator (or window) where the film sensitivity or ASA rating may be set. There is also a scale with numbers that correspond to those that appear on the microammeter dial. When a light reading is taken, the number indicated by the needle is noted and the calculator is rotated manually until the appropriate pointer is aligned with the corresponding number on the calculator scale. Finally, there is a scale that contains the standard series of f-stop numbers (i.e., f-1, f-1.4, f-2, f-2.8, f-4, f-5.6, f-8, f-11, f-16, f-22, f-32, f-45, f-64, f-90,

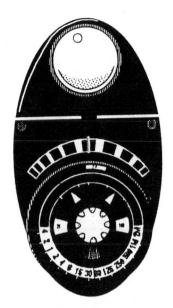

FIGURE 7.4 Sekonic L-398 incident light meter.

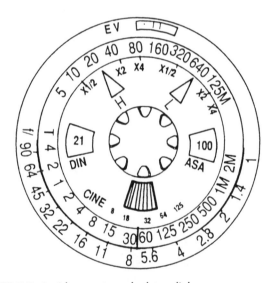

FIGURE 7.5 Incident meter calculator dial.

etc.). This aperture scale rotates in direct proximity around a scale that is inscribed with shutter speed numbers. Beginning with long exposure times of perhaps 60 seconds, these numerals proceed in increments equal to half the preceding time (30 seconds, 15 seconds, 8 seconds, 4 seconds, 2 seconds), move to one second in the middle of the scale, and then continue in fractions of a second. Fractions are usually indicated by a small slanted line. The series proceeds with reduced exposure times that halve the preceding exposure time (e.g., ½ second, ¼ second, 8, 15, 30, 60, 125, 250, 500, 1000). When the calculator dial is set at the point correspond-

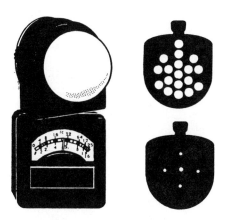

FIGURE 7.6 Spectra Pro Incident Light Meter with two light filter slides.

ing to the needle reading, the f-stop number is located directly adjacent to the shutter speed at which the camera is set. The aperture on the camera lens is then set to this f-stop.

Many incident meters have one or a series of perforated filter slides for adjusting the sensitivity of the light-sensitive cell. A filter is inserted in a slot on the top of the meter to cut down on the light striking the cell. The Sekonic comes with one "high" slide only, for use in exterior and other bright light situations. The Spectra comes equipped with a series of slides, including a ×10, a ×100 (cutting light by those amounts, respectively, for bright light applications), and various ASA-rated slides (see Figure 7.6).

The ASA slides may be used when shooting sync sound motion pictures (when a 1/48 or 1/50 shutter speed is constant). Just insert the appropriate ASA slide for convenient, calculation-free readings directly from the meter.

The advantage of using the incident meter is that a dark object in the scene will be rendered dark on the film, a white object rendered white, and a 36% flesh tone will reproduce on film as a 36% flesh tone, without the need of using a gray card. Consistent and accurate flesh tones are one important way of recognizing correct exposure; for that purpose, no other type of exposure meter will give more accurate readings than the incident meter. The incident meter does

have some disadvantages. It cannot distinguish the luminance of objects; it would not be a good choice for making readings of the sky, for instance. Also, it is not particularly sensitive in low-light conditions, but it is usually sufficient in all motion picture applications.

Other Incident Meter Uses

The incident meter may also be fitted with a flat, translucent, white disc (a *photodisk* or *lumidisk*) in place of the white dome. The disk, being two-dimensional, provides accurate readings of flat subjects—artwork, signs, and table tops. The disk aids in giving a reading that corresponds accurately to the effective surface illumination based on the angle of incidence to the light source. For readings of this nature, the meter is held with its back against the flat surface, with the disk parallel to it.

In addition to the dome and disk attachments, incident meters may also be fitted with a round filter (*lumigrid* or *photomultiplier*), which changes the incident meter to a reflective meter. However, it is best to use a particular meter for the purpose for which it was expressivly designed.

CARE AND FEEDING OF LIGHT METERS

A light meter is a very sensitive instrument; it should never be handled roughly or dropped. If it is dropped or damaged, the meter should be sent out for re-calibration before it is used again. Manufacturers allow themselves ±1/3 f-stop tolerance in calibration, so be sure to check the repaired meter against others; they may not necessarily be in agreement.

The perforation dimensions in filter slides are calibrated to each individual light meter. Store the light meter with its own slides and don't mix the slides up with another meter's slides. Meters are very possessive in this regard; they don't like their family split up in such ways and may give spurious readings as a result. If slides are lost or mixed up, the meter must be sent in for re-calibration. Also, be sure to keep the photosphere and disk free of dust and dirt, as the translucent plastic may discolor or darken with age. If this happens, the meter must be re-calibrated.

Self-Study

■ QUESTIONS

1. The amount of power consumed by a source is measured in _____.
   a. watts
   b. lumens
   c. footcandles

C

2. Incident light is measured in _____ .
   a. watts
   b. lumens
   c. footcandles

3. A subject that receives 160 footcandles at 5 feet from a specular source will receive _____ footcandles at 10 feet.
   a. 20
   b. 40
   c. 80

4. The correct way to use an incident meter for general readings of three-dimensional subjects is to use it with the _____ in place.
   a. lumisphere (photosphere)
   b. lumidisk (photodisk)
   c. photomultiplier

5. The easiest way to take general, incident readings is to point the light-sensitive selenium cell toward _____ .
   a. the shadowed side of the subject
   b. the highlighted side of the subject
   c. the camera

6. The 18% card is *never* used to take light readings with the _____ .
   a. incident meter
   b. spot meter
   c. TTL meter

7. When using an incident meter with precalibrated EI filter slides for calculation-free readings, you must shoot with a shutter speed of _____ .
   a. 1/50 second
   b. 1/30 second
   c. 1/125 second

8. While the footcandle is the prime measurement of luminous intensity in the United States, the meter-candle or _____ is commonly used by the rest of the world and the scientific community.
   a. lumen
   b. footlambert
   c. lux

9. A disadvantage of selenium cell meters is their _____ .
   a. relative insensitivity to low light
   b. need for a power source (battery)
   c. tendency to lag in diverse lighting situations

10. An object that is exactly 13.5 feet from a radiating light source receives 60 footcandles of light. If that object is placed 4.5 feet from the source it would receive _____ footcandles of light.
   a. 540
   b. 180
   c. 30

■ ANSWERS

1. a. The amount of power consumed by a source is measured in watts.

2. c. Incident light is measured in footcandles.

3. b. Incident light changes inversely to the square of the change of the distance between the light source and the subject. It might seem that doubling the distance between the source and the subject would have the light to 80 footcandles, but light radiates outward in three dimensions from a source. The same light that evenly illuminates a 1-foot square surface spreads out at twice the distance to cover an area four times as large. A 1-foot square surface thus receives one-quarter of its original light. One quarter of 160 is 40.

4. a. The proper method fot taking incident light readings of three-dimensional objects is with the dome-shaped lumisphere in place. The dome mimics a three-dimensional object, such as a face, and averages the light that strikes it from many angles. The flat lumidisk, however, receives only a portion of light and is adapted to readings of flat surfaces. The photomultiplier converts the incident meter into a reflected meter.

5. c. The incident meter is designed to read incident light and should be pointed away from the reflective subject, in the case of general exposure readings, toward the camera. A reflected light meter must be used to take readings of shadows and highlights.

6. a. The gray card, a surface of known reflectance, is a useful tool to use in conjunction with spot meters, TTL meters, and other reflected light meters. Incident light meters, on the other hand, are not used to read reflective surfaces; thus, a gray card is not useful in this case.

7. a. Many incident meters, such as those made by Spectra, have a series of slides that enable *filmmakers* to make direct exposure readings. The slides are designed to be used with a motion picture that uses a shutter speed of 1/50 second. If you select any other shutter speed, you must calculate the proper exposure with the meter's exposure dial.

8. c. The meter-candle, or lux, is the standard measure of incident light in the scientific community and most of the world (10.76 lux = 1 footcandle, the USA standard). The lumen measures luminous intensity and the footlambert is a measure of reflected light.

9. a. Light meters that incorporate a photovoltaic selenium cell need no batteries and are relatively free from the lag that affects the CdS cells. Unfortunately, selenium cell meters are relatively unresponsive in very low-light conditions.

10. a. Remember, the intensity of light measured at a surface is inversely proportional to the square of the distance between the source and the surface measured. First determine the degree of change—4.5 feet is three times closer than 13.5 feet (13.5/4.5 = 3) and three squared is nine. The light intensity, 60 footcandles, times the change in distance squared, which is 9 feet, equals 540 footcandles.

■ PROJECT 7.1: INTERPRETING REFLECTED METER READINGS

Purpose:

To become familiar with the use of the reflected light meter, to experience the effect of the reflected light meter in various lighting situations, and to learn how to correct the exposure recommendation given by the reflected light meter in certain lighting situations.

Materials Needed:

camera and film
camera log (see Figure 7.7) and pencil
reflected light meter (either built-in or hand-held)
model

The reflected light meter is one of the most frequently used camera accessories. It is also one of the most frequently misused. In this project, you will find out what the reflected light meter will and will not do. The reflected light meter will average any scene into a middle-gray tone—actually an 18% reflectance gray. Whether the subject is dark or light, the reflected light meter will indicate the best exposure to render the subject middle gray. Thus, if the subject is darker or lighter than middle gray, the photographer must manually adjust the reflected light meter recommendation to obtain the correct exposure.

Procedure:

1. Load the camera with film and set the correct EI number on the camera light meter.
2. Find a medium-gray wall—one that is neither dark nor very light. It can be colored, but make sure the color is not too dark or light. The wall should be lit by bright sunlight.
3. Expose the model standing against the wall. Have the model stand against the wall and photograph from about 10 feet away with a normal lens. Meter from the camera position and expose one frame at the meter reading. Make

CAMERA LOG	PROJECT				FILM TYPE:	
EXPOSURE.	GROUP #	F/STOP	SH. SPD.	FILTER USED	LIGHT RATIO	SHOT DESCRIPTION

FIGURE 7.7 Camera log.

sure no sky is included in either the meter reading or the photograph. Note the frame number in the camera log and label it "gray wall."

4. Locate a dark wall; dark bricks or a darkly painted wall will do quite well. Ensure the wall is lit by bright sunlight.
5. Expose the model against the wall. Have the model stand against the wall and photograph from about 10 feet away with a normal lens. Meter from the camera position. Make sure no sky is included in either the meter reading or the photograph. Make exposure by the meter recommendation. Note the frame number in the camera log and label it "dark wall—meter reading."
6. Expose the model against the dark wall changing the exposure. Using the same dark wall, make an exposure *1 stop less* than that indicated by the meter; mark this frame in the camera log as "dark wall—1 stop." Repeat the

procedure, but make an exposure *2 stops less* than that indicated by the meter; mark this frame "dark wall—2 stops."

7. Locate a light wall; a wall that has been painted white is ideal. Ensure the wall is lit by bright sunlight.

8. Expose the model against the wall. Use the same procedures as detailed in Step #6; mark this frame "light wall."

9. Expose the model against the light wall changing the exposure. Using the same light wall, make an exposure *1 stop more* than that indicated by the meter; mark this frame "light wall + 1 stop." Repeat this procedure, but make an exposure *2 stops more* than that indicated by the meter; mark this frame "light wall + 2 stops."

10. Compare each slide with the appropriate entry in the camera log. Notice that the exposure recommended by the meter was correct only for the gray wall. Observe how dark or light subjects must be exposed. Also note how a figure against a light or dark background is rendered at various exposures.

The reflected light meter is a tool for measuring luminance. It averages all light striking its photosensitive cell and suggests exposures based on the assumption that it is reading a subject that reflects 18% of all light striking it. Since the meter does not take into account variances in a subject's relative reflectance or the presence of incident light sources in its field of reception (such as open sky), the resulting reading must always be interpreted by the photographer and, if necessary, adjusted accordingly.

CHAPTER EIGHT

Manipulating Light: Direction and Balance

INTRODUCTION

The direction of the light within a scene will suggest the time of day, the type of location, and the mood of that scene. It will also model the objects within a scene, bringing out their shape and texture, or perhaps intentionally *not* bringing out their shape and texture. The bright, cheery daytime dining room may become a sinister, shadowy nighttime scene by changing the placement of just a few lights.

THE KEY LIGHT AND KEY LIGHT PLACEMENT

The primary source of illumination in any given scene, which establishes the perceived direction and character of the light, is called the *key light*. Key light placement is always dictated by the effect desired by the cinematographer.

There are three important questions to consider when setting key light:

front-back: Which side of the subject will be illuminated?
high-low: Should the light strike the subject from a high or low angle?
hard-soft: Should the light be directional or diffused?

A traditional starting point for key light placement for close-ups is about 45° left or right from the camera and from 30–45° above the floor (see Figure 8.1). The cinematographer will more often put it elsewhere, however, depending on the mood and location of the scene. Another rule of thumb dictates that the key light come from outside the actor's look. In other words, if the actor is looking off-camera (usually the case in narrative films), the key should come from the other side of his line of sight so that the actor is looking between the key light and the camera.

This means that the "short" side of the actor's face will be highlighted, while the broad side of his face will be in shadow. The traditional cheek patch is often used as a guide to the best modeling position for the key light (see Figure 8.2). This triangle of light cast just under the eye on the fill side of the face is sometimes called the *Rembrandt patch,* as it appears in many of the Flemish painter's portraits. *Modeling* refers to the pattern of light and shadows that describe the shapes of the head and face.

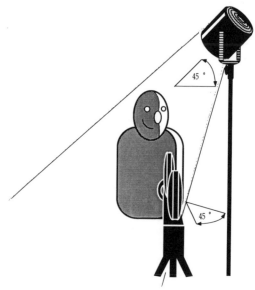

FIGURE 8.1 A traditional starting point for placing the key light is outside the gaze of the subject (about 45° from the camera axis) and about 45° from the floor.

FIGURE 8.2 The triangular cheek patch on the shaded side of a subject's face is a starting point for key light placement in traditional Rembrandt lighting.

Front-Back Key Placement

Direct front lighting gives no distinct modeling, as all shadows are thrown directly behind the subject. A common example of such lighting can be seen in snapshots taken with a camera-mounted flash. Lighting of this kind tends to look harsh, flat, and dull. Except for special effects, this type of lighting is generally unsatisfactory for people and is used only in situations where shadows may interfere with the scene.

As the key light is moved to one side, shadows become more pronounced and the shape of the subject begins to emerge (see Figure 8.3). When the angle approaches 90° from the camera, strong lines and highly defined features become apparent.

When the light moves behind the imaginary 90° line, the front of the subject is predominantly in shadow. This key position is good for creating nighttime effects. When the light is placed directly behind, the subject is seen in silhouette, with only a bright rim of detail remaining. This rim light distinctly separates subjects from the background and produces a halo effect.

High-Low Key Placement

Naturalistic lighting usually dictates that the primary light source, like the sun, should emanate from above the subject. However, too-high frontal key light produces unpleasant nose and eyesocket shadows that are reminiscent of harsh, midday sunlight.

When the key light is moved below a subject's eye level, the resulting upward shadows produce an unnatural, sinister effect. This low-angle lighting, used for mysterious or supernatural effects, is easily exaggerated and overdone.

Top light is used to simulate skylight or overhead practical fixtures and is not usually considered a key light placement, but is an overall illumination booster or fill light. *Bottom light* is useful in product photography, but is seldom used in film lighting.

Hard-Soft Key Quality

When the surfaces of objects and walls are illuminated by lights placed near the camera, the surfaces will appear even and flat. As the angle of incidence approaches 90° from the camera, the texture of a surface becomes more apparent and exaggerated. Textures, shapes, and variations in backgrounds all stand in sharp relief when illuminated by strongly angled or raking light (see Figure 8.4).

When illuminating people, only one key light is usually used for a given subject or position. When two or more hard lights overlap on a person's face and cast double and triple shadows, the lighting becomes distracting and unpleasant. This is why shadows are lightened and softened by large, diffused fill lights. Only when placed more than 90° from the camera and behind the subject do multiple hard lights have a useful role in lighting the subject.

The rules regarding key light placement are often ignored

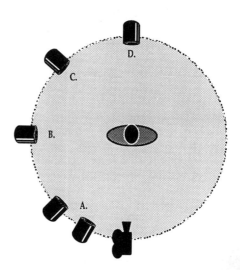

FIGURE 8.3 The traditional starting point for key light placement is between 30° and 45° off the camera axis (A). As the angle becomes more extreme, texture is exaggerated as the side light rakes across the surface; this side light is most extreme when the key light strikes the subject at an angle perpendicular to the camera axis (B). When the light angle exceeds 90 degrees from the camera, the light no longer illuminates the subject as a key and effectively becomes a kicker (C) at around 130° or a straight back light (D) at 180°.

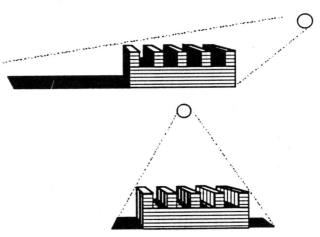

FIGURE 8.4 Raking light strikes from the side and emphasizes texture.

depending on the effect and mood desired, the features of the actor, the set location and topography, and the supposed time of day.

BALANCE

A single light may be powerful enough to illuminate a scene and provide the proper modeling of a subject, but there are other factors to be considered. Film and video are limited in their ability to reproduce a wide range of light and dark values. Panchromatic (black-and-white) film may have a tolerance range from white to black of about 8 stops, while color film can handle about 6 stops. Video-imaging systems can handle at most a range of slightly more than 5 stops. In comparison, the human eye can handle more than 20 stops.

The reflectance of objects plays an important part in the contrast ratio within a given scene. Few scenes contain a 100% white reflector and a 0% black reflector. Therefore, a white house may be only 5 stops brighter than a black pole when both are illuminated by sun at the same angle. The additional problem of shadows causes black details to drop below the acceptable exposure range.

The problem of light balance is keeping the contrast range within the film's latitude while allowing for directionality, interest, and shadows. The balance of lights, called the *lighting ratio*, is adjusted according to four variables:

recording medium
contrast within the scene itself
relative size of the shot
the desired effect

The first variable is the recording medium. All film stocks have distinct characteristics, whether negative, positive, black-and-white, or color. For instance, a reversal color film has less latitude and is more prone to contrast than a negative black-and-white stock. Video has even less latitude and little tolerance for high-contrast lighting situations.

The second variable is the inherent contrast of the scene itself. Exterior and interior scenes can vary widely in colors and values of gray. In an interior location, there may be dark furniture, white walls, and bright windows. In such a case, lighting ratios should be narrow, for less contrast. The same lighting ratio applies when shooting a medium shot of a man in a white shirt and a black suit. This is why the brightness of the colors selected for the set, as well as actor's clothing, should be controlled for photography. If all the objects within the scene are of controlled reflectance, then more dramatic lighting may be used without sacrificing too much detail.

The third variable of lighting ratio is the relative size and the respective shadow predominance of the shot. In an exterior long shot, for example, dark shadows beneath a distant person's chin are of little consequence. However, if the person moves in closely and stops in close-up, the shadows become a predominant element in the scene.

In close-ups of people, shadows must be filled in with reflectors or fill lights. In practice, the key light (or lights) is usually set first, each area of the set is given the proper illumination, and any obvious double shadows eliminated.

Large softlights are then placed near the camera, if possible, so that any shadows they create will fall behind the subject. The amount of fill light is adjusted to bring the shadows to the desired exposure range. This lighting ratio is expressed as 2:1, 3:1, 4:1, and so forth. A 2:1 ratio means that the fill light alone is one half as bright as the fill and key light together, a difference of 1 stop.

Measuring the Lighting Ratio

The lighting ratio is measured with an incident light meter or with a reflected light meter and 18% reflectance gray card. When the key light is placed less than 90° from the camera axis, use the incident meter at the subject's position to read the combined intensities of key and fill. This combination is the brightest, total key illumination on the subject. Next, block out the key light and allow the fill light to strike the meter's dome (see Figure 8.5). If you are using a reflected meter and gray card, try blocking the key with your body or simply turn the key off.

When the key light is more than 90° from the camera axis, the key and fill will no longer strike the same surfaces and will not combine for greater brightness on the subject. Simply read the key and the fill separately (see Figure 8.6).

The ratio can be read in footcandles or f-stops. If the desired ratio is 4:1 and the key-plus-fill-combined reading is 500 footcandles or, say, f-5.6, then the fill light should be set so that by itself it reads 125 footcandles or f-2.8. Remember that a ratio of 3:1 means a difference of 1.5 (not 3!) f-stops.

A contrast-viewing filter for panchromatic or color film is helpful for judging lighting ratios, but the properly used incident light meter is still the most accurate way to place the lights. Even so, it is important to remember that even a

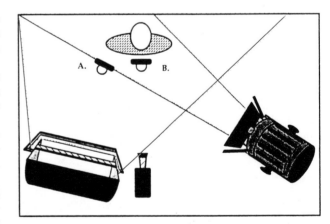

FIGURE 8.5 Measuring the lighting ratio. First read the fill light only by pointing the incident meter dome directly at the fill fixture; block any extraneous key light with your hand. Next, hold the meter directly in front of the subject where the key and fill overlap, and take a reading while pointing the dome at the camera. Compare the two readings—this is the lighting ratio.

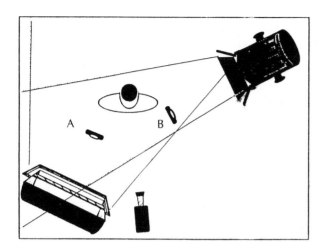

FIGURE 8.6 Reading the key and fill separately. When key and fill lights do not overlap, read each by itself using an incident meter with the white disk instead of the dome.

perfect ratio can be rendered too flat or contrasty by an improper exposure, out-of-date film stock, or faulty processing.

THE SEPARATION LIGHT

Separation light, also called *backlight*, is the third important light used in most lighting setups. Because this kind of lighting is often unmotivated (not justified by the apparent light in a scene), some cinematographers opt not to use backlight. In most instances, however, it is used for all kinds of photography—day, night, mystery, high-key, and low-key. Backlight adds a glistening, three-dimensional quality to the subject. Without it, high-key scenes may look flat and dull, and in low-key and night scenes the subject tends to fade away into the background.

A backlight positioned above and behind the actor, illuminating the top of the shoulders and head, is sometimes called a *hair light*. Another variation on the backlight is the *kicker light*, which is positioned about 135° from the camera and opposite the key light. It is often placed closer to the floor than the backlight. A low-set kicker that creates a bright rim on the cheek, neck, and sleeve is often called a *cheek light*.

Relatively hard light sources, like the spotlights used for key lights, are used for separation light. They are usually arranged to cover the entire blocking area of a set with even illumination, so that the actors are backlit at all times.

Separation lights are usually set to about the same illumination as the key light—and sometimes even higher. Be sure to turn off (or shield the light from) the backlight when taking light readings for fill and key lights, in order to prevent false readings. The backlight does not illuminate the surface facing the camera and therefore does not affect the key-to-fill lighting ratio and film exposure.

As mentioned earlier, the use of high backlights and low kickers depends upon the situation; sometimes one, both, or neither are employed. Their use is up to the director of photography.

THE BACKGROUND LIGHT

The lighting discussed so far has been concerned with the illumination of the subjects or actors within the set. But when the set walls, background, or floors are visible elements in the composition of a shot, they must be given lighting consideration as well.

The quantity of illumination for backgrounds depends on two factors—the reflective quality and color brightness of the background itself, and the desired mood or effect of the lighting. Strong or saturated colors are usually avoided in set wall finishes, because they tend to overpower most subjects. In brightly painted locations where the background cannot be controlled, background illumination may have to be kept very low to avoid distractions. Locations with white walls often pick up enough illumination from stray key and fill lighting and do not need additional illumination. In fact, when the subject is very near a white wall, it is difficult to keep the wall from getting too "hot" and overexposing the film. As the desired mood of the shot is the primary concern, overlighting the background by 2 or 3 stops and washing out detail altogether may be just right for certain effects. For night and low-key effects, keep extraneous light off the background and control exposure carefully so that only a few textures and details are revealed.

It is difficult to be specific about suggested quantities of light for backgrounds, since the variables are so broad. Generally speaking, however, the ratios between the foreground or subject illumination and the background illumination are much like the ratios between key and fill light when backgrounds are of mid-range color values. For long shots of general subjects with normal contrast and light-colored backgrounds, a ratio of 4:1 between the total illumination on the subject and the total illumination of the background is typical. Ordinarily, the background illumination is not increased for close-ups. The exception to this is a low-key situation when background illumination is so low that only a few highlights are revealed in the long shot. Switch to a close-up and the background will go completely black, unless the angle includes a few of these background highlights. Chances are that the close-up will be more interesting if a few of these highlights are deliberately included, either by careful angle selection or lighting adjustment.

The direction of lighting for backgrounds is usually the same as the general key light direction. Shadows cast by picture frames, furniture, and doors should fall in the same direction as those on the actor's face and cast by other subjects in the scene. Background lights are placed near the sides of the set beyond the key light positions or clamped to the tops of the adjacent set walls or both. Small lights may sometimes be hidden behind furniture or outside of open doorways, but they must be controlled carefully so that no stray hot spots appear on door frames, walls, or furniture.

Location walls and backgrounds should be illuminated with varying tonal areas to avoid the tendency of walls to reproduce as the visually dull surfaces they often are. Let walls get slightly darker at the top, bottom, and in the corners. Barndoors should be used to keep excess light off parts of the walls. Use focused spotlights to highlight paintings on the wall, tables, and dark furniture. Use an incident meter to measure light intensity at illuminated walls and surfaces. For this purpose, the meter should be fitted with the flat disk receptor.

When practicals (visible sources of light such as table lamps) appear in a shot, hang a small focused spot to create a circle of light on the adjacent wall or table. The light bulb in the lamp should provide just enough intensity to make the shade appear bright. But it will probably not cause the desired extra brightness on the surrounding surfaces, so the additional spotlight is added. The illumination of highlight areas such as this should be about the same as the foreground or subject illumination. They are easily checked with a reflected light meter.

Cycloramas are backgrounds with curved corners and sloping bottoms that eliminate visible floor edges. Subjects photographed before such a backdrop will appear as if floating in space; this is sometimes called the *limbo effect.* This effect can also be achieved with seamless paper, available in rolls measuring up to 12 × 100ft. When using a cyc or seamless paper backdrop, illumination is usually a problem of providing extremely even and flat lighting or of breaking up the flatness and providing a sort of abstract interest behind the subject.

The smooth, even lighting of cycloramas is usually achieved by using special lighting instruments called *sky pans* and *striplights.* These instruments are hung every few feet across the entire width of the background and several feet away from the top, front edge so that they may be tilted down to illuminate the entire surface. When the background is serving as a "sky" seen through set windows or behind scenery, the pans or striplights can be placed along the bottom edge and sides as well.

The illumination on large, flat backdrops and walls is often broken up into a mottled shadow effect by directing the light through a cookie. Shadows that appear to be cast by foliage, windows, and venetian blinds are often created through the use of cookies. The cookie is most effective when placed in front of a hard light source. Size and intensity of the shadow pattern can be adjusted by moving the cookie between the light source and the surface. A wide variety of small cookies (called gobos or patterns) are commercially available for use in ellipsoidal fixtures. The pattern slides into a slot behind the shutter and can be focused by moving the front lens element of the fixture in or out.

Self-Study

■ QUESTIONS

1. A 1K is set up 8 feet from John's face; in another scene, Janet's face is lit by another identical 1K 11 feet away. The brighter face will be lighter by _____ stop.
   a. 1
   b. a ½
   c. a ⅓
2. Hair light, kicker light, and cheek light are all variants of _____.
   a. separation light
   b. key light
   c. background light
3. Lighting fixtures included within a shot are called _____.
   a. practicals
   b. luminaires
   c. lights
4. In most cases, the preferred fixture for fill light is a _____.
   a. Fresnel
   b. PAR
   c. softlight

5. An 8:1 light ratio indicates a difference of _____ stops between the fill and the key sides of a subject's face.
   a. 3
   b. 4
   c. 8

6. If two, identical, 1000-watt fixtures are set up as shown in Figure 8.7, a _____ lighting ratio will be achieved.
   a. 2:1
   b. 3:1
   c. 1:1

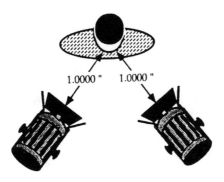

1.0000 "   1.0000 "

FIGURE 8.7

7. If an incident meter reads f-4 for the fill and f-22 for the fill-plus-key, what is the lighting ratio?
   a. 8:1
   b. 16:1
   c. 32:1

8. When reading light ratios, take the reading for the shaded side by pointing the dome directly at the fill light and the reading for the highlight side by pointing the dome at the _____.
   a. key light
   b. camera
   c. highlight

9. If the key and fill light do not overlap, it is best to read them separately with the _____ inserted in the incident light meter.
   a. photomultiplier
   b. photodisk
   c. EI slide

10. The key/fill lighting configuration in Figure 8.8 provides a _____ lighting ratio.
   a. 1:3
   b. 1:4
   c. 1:5

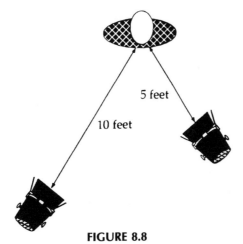

5 feet

10 feet

FIGURE 8.8

■ ANSWERS

1. a. The inverse square law states that the intensity of incident light changes inversely to the square of the change in distance between the source and the subject. To find the difference in distance, divide the greater distance, 11 feet, by the shorter distance, 8 feet. The greater distance is 1.375 times the lesser distance. The change in distance squared is 1.89 or nearly 2 times. This means that the amount of light on John is double that on Janet's face, a 1-stop increase.

2. a. Hair, kicker, and cheek lights are different kinds of separation lights, used primarily to separate a subject from its background. When light strikes a subject from behind in this manner, it serves as an effects light, rather than as a true key source. Background light is used to illuminate props, walls, and backdrops behind the subject.

3. a. Practicals are working lighting fixtures that appear within a scene as props. *Light* is a loose term meaning any lighting fixture as well as the illumination it emits. A luminaire is a professional lighting fixture such as a Fresnel spotlight.

4. c. The softlight, with its wraparound, nearly shadowless illumination, is the most logical choice for fill light, which should bring up shaded areas without casting visible shadows of its own. The Fresnel can be used as fill, but its directional beam casts distinct shadows. The PAR throws an even harder beam of light. Any spot can be diffused or used as a bounce source that produces an appropriately soft illumination.

5. a. A 1-stop increase is equal to a doubling of light intensity; a 1-stop decrease is a halving of light intensity. An 8:1 lighting ratio is one in which the highlight is eight times or 3 stops (doublings of light intensity) brighter than the shadow. One stop = $2\times$, two stops = $4\times$, three stops = $8\times$.

6. a. The two fixtures are equally bright and set at equal distances from the subject. Shouldn't they make for a 1:1 ratio? No, because the lighting ratio is based on the difference between the brightest highlight where the key and fill light *overlap,* and the fill light alone. The combined intensity of two equally bright sources will be double the light from one of the sources and results in a lighting ratio of 2:1.

7. c. The difference between f-4 and f-22 is 5 stops. Five stops equals five doublings of the fill intensity—2, 4, 8, 16, 32. Therefore, the lighting ratio of key-plus-fill to fill is 32:1.

8. b. When reading key and fill together, point the incident light meter directly at the camera lens to ensure you are reading the sum total of light that the camera will register.

9. b. Read flat areas, such as fill- and key-lit areas, that do not overlap with the flat, white, translucent photodisk in place of the dome. The photodisk measures a narrower angle of acceptance than the dome and is not as susceptible to ambient light flaring. The photomultiplier is used to convert the incident meter into a reflected light meter and should not be used for reading incident light ratios. EI slides are used for making direct, calculation-free exposure readings with a motion picture camera.

10. c. This lighting ratio question is also an inverse square law problem. Two identical lights are set up—one twice the distance from the subject as the other. If the light from both did not overlap, the light would be 4 times brighter on one side than the other. The lamp farther from the subject is the fill, adding its single strength illumination to the 4 times brigher key for a combined key-plus-fill light of 5 to 1 of the fill alone.

■ PROJECT 8.1: SETTING LIGHT RATIOS

Purpose:

To gain experience using the incident light meter to determine lighting ratios.

Materials Needed:

model
room with medium-size window

35mm camera with manual exposure control
one roll EI 100 film
incident light meter
tripod
one light kit or three directional fixtures
one softlight
cukaloris
any C-stands and gobos you may need
filter book or #85 gel sheeting for window
accessories as needed (gaffer tape, diffision material, clothespins, etc.)
camera log (see Figure 8.9) and pen

CAMERA LOG	PROJECT				FILM TYPE:	
EXPOSURE.	GROUP #	F/STOP	SH. SPD.	FILTER USED	LIGHT RATIO	SHOT DESCRIPTION

FIGURE 8.9 Camera log.

Procedure:

1. Pose your subject indoors. Control extraneous light; pull all shades. Seat subject at least 4 feet before a suitable background, mount the camera on a tripod, and frame the picture as a ¾-angle shot for all compositions. All you need is one good exposure of each of the six setups. You have four exposures to use for each of the six compositions. Note exposure number, subject, aperture, shutter speed, location, time of day, and lighting ratio in the camera log.
2. For exposures 1–8, light the subject using only one lighting fixture of your choice. Shoot a medium shot with a 1:1 ratio. Reshoot the same scene using one light and a 2:1 ratio.
3. For exposures 8–16, pose the subject next to a window so that the light illuminates the short side of the face. Use window light as key and one light fixture as fill. Photograph the model in a medium shot with a 16:1 and then an 8:1 ratio. Remember to use gobos, nets, scrims, and gels as needed.
4. For exposures 17–24, move the model away from the window. Position the lights in a key/fill/separation light configuration and set the key so that it illuminates the short side of the face. Use a cookie and background light to cast an interesting pattern across the scene. Light should appear natural, like filtered daylight. Shoot a full shot with a 6:1 ratio. Frame the subject in a close-up and shoot with a 4:1 ratio.

Evaluating the Results:

When you are finished, you should have six different portraits photographed under diffused and direct illumination, in lighting ratios of 1:1, 2:1, 4:1, 6:1, 8:1, and 16:1. All that is required is one properly exposed, well-lit-picture from each grouping—six portraits. Which of the six setups has the most evocative lighting? Which is the most flattering to the model? Which is the least flattering? Which setups seem to be most successful?

KEY for LIGHTING PLOTS

Lowell Tota-light

1K Fresnel

2K Fresnel

5K Fresnel

200w Pepper

Skypan

Pro-light

650w Compact

Broad or Nook

Softlight

Video Camera

Film Camera

Subjects

Scrim

Gel

Flicker Stick

Butterfly/Silk

Cookie

Shiny Board

Foam Core or Show Card

Flag

CHAPTER NINE

Lighting Concepts in Practice

INTRODUCTION

In Chapters 1–8 we discussed the science of light and its properties—quality, intensity, color temperature, direction, and balance. The following chapters explore the art, craft, and practice of motion picture and television lighting. Since the emphasis here is on *practice*, you will find no self-study questions in Chapters 9, 10, and 11. These chapters have been augmented with more projects, which you will find interspersed throughout each chapter.

The projects you will encounter in this chapter are all basic lighting setups that may be used for a variety of situations. They are meant to be created in any medium-size room with a minimum of instruments. Because schools and production units vary widely in terms of available lighting equipment, these setups have been kept very elementary. Many effective lighting plans can be derived from these models; however, these and other lighting plans in this book are not meant to be formulas. Try these setups a few times as designed and then vary them; change the combinations and configurations for the best effect. Then forget them and experiment on your own. The best approach to film and video lighting, as with all art, is to go with your own intuition.

LIGHTING STYLES

The narrative, dramatic, and informative traditions of motion pictures and television owe much to literature, theater, and radio. The conventions of film and video lighting, however, derive from the visual arts, primarily from discoveries made long ago by the old masters of traditional oil painting. Thus, all lighting for film and video draws from one of three distinct styles taken from representational painting—high-key lighting, low-key lighting, and modulated value lighting.

High-Key Lighting

A high-key scene is one that appears predominantly bright overall. High-key lighting can be seen in the paintings of Franz Hals and Hans Holbein, and in most musicals and comedies produced before the 1970s. Most multicamera television programs taped before a live audience also use high-key lighting. This kind of lighting, which may be created with directional or diffused sources, features strong, even illumination on both subject and background, bright highlights, and relatively few shadows.

Low-Key Lighting

Other painters, notably Caravaggio and Rembrandt, developed a style that enhanced the three-dimensional qualities of their subjects by using contrasting tones of highlight and shadow. Their subjects were often illuminated in sharp relief against dark backgrounds. This type of painting, called *chiaroscuro* (pronounced key-AR-oh-skur-oh), literally *light-dark*, uses directional lighting that emphasizes deep shadows and extreme contrasts; it is the antecedent to film and television low-key lighting. Detective movies, mysteries, and horror films customarily use low-key lighting to great effect, as does the entire genre known as *film noir* (literally, *black film*). Since the 1960s, low-key lighting techniques have crept into other genres as well, including comedies, love stories, and action films.

Modulated Value Lighting

Much natural interior lighting is neither high- nor low-key, but instead reflects a continuum of modulated medium values. Modulated value lighting is often diffused or diffused directional lighting. Daytime window light is a good source of modulated value lighting; an excellent example of this is seen in the interior scenes painted by the Dutch painter Vermeer van Delft. In these paintings, the lighting is soft, but directional, and is nearly always clearly justified or motivated by the light emanating from an open window; few values are extremely dark or bright.

Often, in narrative films, interior lighting appears motivated by sunlight that shines directly through windows to form hard, rhomboid patterns on adjoining walls. This kind of lighting appears frequently in paintings by the American artist Edward Hopper. In the real world, this lighting occurs only for brief periods during the very early morning and very late afternoon (if there are no buildings or trees outside to block it). Most of the day, the sun is so high overhead that its direct rays reach only small areas of floor. Despite this fact, most contemporary films and television shows nearly always depict interior daylight scenes illuminated by steeply raking crosslight, because it is evocative and tends to look the most realistic.

■ PROJECT 9.1: THREE STYLES FOR MOTIVATED INTERIOR WINDOW LIGHTING

Purpose:

To create modulated value, high-key, and low-key window lighting in a single environment.

Materials Needed:

a medium-size room with one window
model
assistant
video camcorder or camera and VCR
tripod
incident meter for determining light ratios
one 1000-watt or 650-watt focusable fixture (a Fresnel such as a baby is ideal) with barndoors and stand
one softlight or one broad fixture (a Tota-light will do)
one shiny board (or equivalent) with stand
one C-stand
one flag
one scrim or net
one diffusion sheet, such as tracing paper, a sheet, or a plastic shower curtain liner, to cover the window
one blue gel to filter the spotlight
two sandbags
one grounded, AC extension cable
one 30 × 40-inch foam core sheet or show card
black wrap
cukaloris (optional)
accessories as needed (gaffer tape, gels, clothespins, etc.)

Procedure:

In this project, the emphasis is on natural, motivated window lighting. You will create three different effects using the same interior and motivation direction.

1. *Vermeer Lighting (diffused, directional, modulated value lighting)*—In the mid-daylight hours (10:00 AM–3:00 PM), pose a figure standing by an open window. Incoming daylight should be diffused and should define the model in crosslight. If the sun is shining in directly, cover the window with tracing paper or Roscoscrim. Fasten the paper or scrim with gaffer tape to the exterior window frame to ensure that the light will be diffused. Your setup should look like the one depicted in Figure 9.1. If the contrast is high, fill in some of the shadows with a reflector card mounted on a C-stand.

2. *Edward Hopper Lighting (direct, high-key window sunlight)*—In Hopper's paintings, direct sunlight often cuts through tall windows to define figures in sharp relief for a high-key effect. Pose the model as in step #1. In this exercise, you will want to illuminate the model in hard sunlight. Since it is difficult, if not impossible, to wait until the sun is just right, you will be cheating the effect.

   Arcs, HMIs, and PAR-FAY clusters are the only artificial sources that can begin to compete with the intensity of daylight. A shiny board, however, will give you the power of the sun itself. Set up a reflector board outside the window to catch the sun's rays and reflect them through the window (see Figure 9.2). Have an assistant aim the board to keep the sun reflecting through the window. Dim the strong light somewhat by using a slip-on reflector net and fill in the high-contrast light on the model by using a card or even a softlight.

3. *Caravaggio Lighting (low-key chiaroscuro lighting)*—This kind of lighting emphasizes high contrast and shadow for effect. The motivation is the full moon or perhaps an outdoor streetlight. Use the same model blocking as in steps #2 and #3, and set up this shot after the sun goes down. Set up a fixture outside the window and angle the

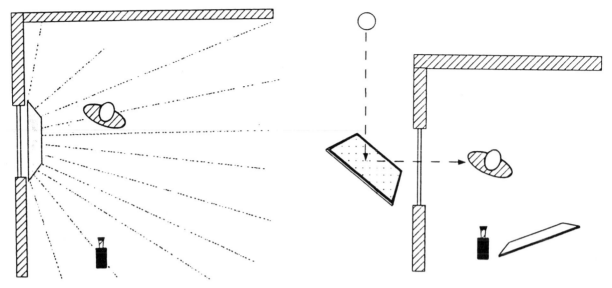

FIGURE 9.1 Vermeer lighting.   **FIGURE 9.2** High-key sunlight.

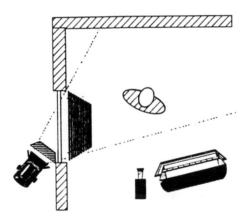

FIGURE 9.3 Low-key night lighting.

fixture in to imitate the steep lighting of the full moon (in this case, clip a blue gel to the barndoors) or street lamp (see Figure 9–3).

If you have to shoot this step during the day for any reason, block out all ambient daylight by covering the window with heavy black plastic garbage bags or duvatyne. Then cut a hole in the plastic that is just big enough for the light to pass through. Set a 1K or 650-watt fixture outside the window to shine through the hole.

If the window is equipped with blinds, produce a convincing film noir effect by pulling the blinds down to break up the light into the familiar bar pattern. If blinds are unavailable, set up a cookie outside the window to imitate the mottled pattern of light filtering through foilage. You may wish to introduce some fill to decrease the lighting ratio. Experimentation will yield the most pleasing effect.

In many interior lighting situations, motivated window lighting is augmented with artificial illumination because window light falloff is generally steep. PAR-FAYs and HMIs are ideal, as they match the color temperature of daylight. If tungsten sources are used, fit the window with CTO or #85 gel, available in 55-in. × 100-ft rolls. The best method is to cut the gel to the window size and tape it to the exterior perimeter of the window frame with gaffer tape where it will not appear in the shot. As an alternative, gelling the tungsten sources to match daylight is less desirable, as it cuts intensity by about 75%.

BASIC LIGHTING CONFIGURATIONS

Lighting plans vary considerably based on the room, the number of subjects, the available equipment, and the effect desired by the director. There are, however, a number of elemental lighting schemes that can be adapted and expanded to cover a wide variety of situations. The basic setups include lighting for one shots (three-point lighting), two-shots (cross-key lighting), and semicontrolled action (360° lighting).

Basic Three-Point Setup

The three-point lighting scheme is the most often taught lighting configuration and the most useful as a starting point for shooting a single subject in a controlled situation, as a close-up, medium shot, or as a documentary-style interview, such as a controlled interview.

The Controlled Interview

Controlled interviews are the staple of informational programs and documentaries. In fact, the "talking head" interview technique works not only for nonnarrative programming, but also for dramatic, nonfiction and fiction feature films (e.g., the entire film *The Thin Blue Line* [Errol Morris, 1988] and parts of *When Harry Met Sally . . .* [Rob Reiner, 1989]).

■ PROJECT 9.2: LIGHTING AN INTERVIEW

Purpose:

To illuminate a single, seated subject.

Materials Needed:

subject
video camcorder or camera and VCR
incident light meter
tripod
three Lowel Tota-lights
one open-faced 650-watt compact fixture (a Lowel Pro-light, Omni-light, or Mole-Richardson teenie will do nicely)
six light stands
four sandbags
four grounded, AC extension cables
three 30 × 40-inch foam core sheets or 48 × 60-inch show cards
black wrap (optional)
cukaloris (optional)
accessories as needed (gaffer tape, diffusion, clothespins, etc.)
camera log and pen

Procedure:

This setup provides three-point, diffused lighting that is quite versatile for interviewing subjects in a controlled environment (see Figure 9.4). Since documentary production seldom allows the space, budget, and power requirements of grids, C-stands, and Fresnel fixtures, this setup has been designed for a minimum of equipment. In this case, our shooting situation includes an interviewer, a camera operator, and a sound person. The interviewer sits immediately to the right and just in front of the camera. Seen through the camera viewfinder, the subject will be speaking to the interviewer and looking camera-right. The key will also be placed on the right side of the camera.

1. Clamp a 30 × 40-inch card onto a C-stand and set up a Tota-light to bounce off its reflective white surface. If you require more light, use a double pin accessory to mount two Tota-lights on the same stand.

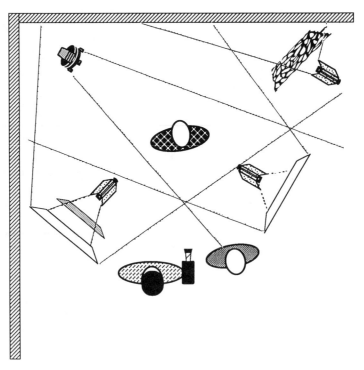

FIGURE 9.4 A lighting plan for controlled interviews.

2. If spill light from the key creates a camera lens flare or otherwise creates problems, flag off the light by positioning another show card between the camera and the fixture. You can also fasten black wrap to the barndoors of the Tota-light using clothespins or fasten the black wrap to the stand itself, using spring clamps, to eliminate the spill.
3. Now you have a diffused, directional key light, which also makes a very nice eye light as well. But since this, alone, usually creates too extreme a lighting ratio for video interviews, you need to set a fill. Do this by setting up a second Tota-light a bit further back from the subject. If the room is not large enough for this, then use one or two layers of ND filter between the lamp and the card to bring down the fill. Spill light from the fill on the ceiling may add some good overall base light.
4. Set the compact fixture high on a stand and aim it to rake across the top of the subject's head and shoulders. You may want to narrow the beam by affixing a snoot made of black wrap. If the source is too bright, scrim it. In this instance, hair light is best kept to a minimum; use just enough to separate the subject from the background.
5. You may decide to highlight the background with another compact. Use a cukaloris to give an interesting mottled effect to an otherwise lifeless back wall.

Cross-Key Lighting

The three-point model is a good starting point for lighting a single subject that will remain stationary, as in an interview. It is often difficult, however, to hold to this kind of approach in real lighting situations that involve more than one subject.

A scene that includes two subjects who are conversing often calls for a cross-key lighting approach. In this configuration, two keys are used, one for each subject. Each light is set so that it keys one subject and backlights the other.

■ PROJECT 9.3: CROSS-KEY LIGHTING

Purpose:

To light a two-shot with a minimum of equipment.

Materials Needed:

a medium-size room
two subjects
video camcorder or camera and VCR
tripod
incident meter for determining light ratios
three teenies with stands
three C-stands
three flags
three full scrims or nets
three half scrims
sandbags for stands
three grounded, AC extension cables
one 30 × 40-inch foam core sheet or show card
black wrap
accessories as needed (gaffer tape, gels, clothespins, etc.)

Procedure:

The two-shot master scene is an essential element of most narrative films. While separate, close-up and reaction one shots offer more lighting control, the two-shot is nearly always necessary to establish a sense of connection between the two actors. Cross-keying is an effective method of lighting this kind of shot. Motivation for most cross-key plans is the practical lights on ceilings or high walls (or streetlamps in outdoor situations).

1. Block the actors positions as in Figure 9.5, so that they face each other in conversation.

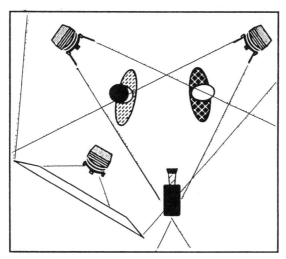

FIGURE 9.5 A simple, cross-key lighting plan.

2. Rig the teenies high behind each subject and angle them to key light one figure, while backlighting the other.
3. Set up a white card on a C-stand near the camera facing the action. Bounce the third teenie off the card to fill in strong shadows left by the high key lights.
4. At this point, you may wish to gel the lights to get more separation. Red gels on the keys and a blue on the fill might suggest a nightclub atmosphere; blue over the keys and amber on the fill would give a warmer, more subtle night look.

Semicontrolled Action

Lighting style depends on the content of the film—that is, the way the film is to be acted and how shots are framed and constructed. Strict adherence to Rembrandt lighting or chiaroscuro techniques is often difficult to maintain with animated subjects. Low-key lighting means pooling light in specific areas and requires actors to limit their movements or else lose the lighting that has been so carefully arranged for them. Documentary-style takes and dramatic sequence shots dictate that subjects and often the camera be allowed to move freely throughout a set. This requires a looser lighting approach designed to give a general high-key illumination over a wide area, including several moving subjects.

■ PROJECT 9.4: 360° LIGHTING

Purpose:

To light a semicontrolled action situation.

Materials Needed:

a medium-size room
three or more subjects
video monitor or camera and VCR
tripod
incident meter for determining light ratios
three broad fixtures (Nooklights, Tota-lights, etc.) or softlights with stands
toughspun or similar diffusion material
sandbags for stands
three grounded, AC extension cables
black wrap
accessories as needed (gaffer tape, gels, clothespins, etc.)

Procedure:

Tightly focused spots are not particularly useful when the action is not controlled. In this case, a broad, overall diffused light is best to provide maximum coverage.

1. Mount three broad fixtures high and angle them down. Aim them into the action area in a roughly 10–2–6 o'clock configuration (see Figure 9.6).

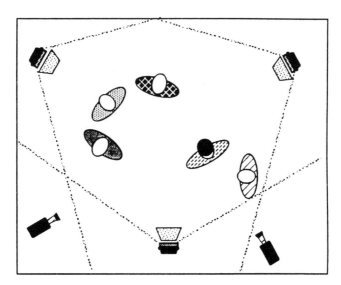

FIGURE 9.6 Lighting for semicontrolled action situations. This configuration allows for several camera angles without the bother of resetting lights.

2. Clip diffusion material to the barndoors to soften the light further. Try to mount the fixtures on top of doors, rafters, or other high mounts to avoid cluttering the floor and field of view with light stands.

    This lighting configuration is useful when the videographer has little time to set lights before the shoot and is quite workable for documentary and nonnarrative situations.

KEY for LIGHTING PLOTS

Lowell Tota-light

1K Fresnel   2K Fresnel   5K Fresnel

200w Pepper

Skypan

Broad or Nook

Softlight

Pro-light   650w Compact

Video Camera

Film Camera

Subjects

Scrim

Gel

Flicker Stick

Butterfly/Silk

Cookie

Shiny Board

Foam Core or Show Card

Flag

CHAPTER TEN

Lighting in the Studio

INTRODUCTION

Before any production begins, the *director* and the *director of photography* (DP) will discuss the script and style or approach to be taken in shooting. The approach will depend a great deal on the mood and character of each scene in the story. As stated earlier, serious drama may employ a largely low-key approach, while comedy is effective in a high-key setting. Realistic narratives may benefit from a modulated value lighting approach. There are no set rules as to the styles to be used in different cases; it is up to the director and the director of photography to choose a style that is most appropriate to their aims.

THE PRODUCTION CREW

The DP is aided by several technicians, including a *camera operator* and a *gaffer*. The DP may also operate a camera on independent and foreign productions; union regulations, however, often preclude this practice in the United States. The operator is in charge of actual camera operation and, in turn, has one or more camera assistants to load camera magazines, regularly inspect the cameras before and after shooting and between takes, pull focus and zoom (adjust focus and focal length for camera lens during a shot), take light readings, and slate takes with a clapper board. The gaffer is the chief electrician on the production and gives instructions to the *best boy* (or first electrical assistant) and several other assistants or *grips* who rig any grids, cables, lights, accessories, generators, and other electrical applications necessary to the production.

On multicamera television shoots, there is no exact equivalent of the cinematographer—lighting is usually handled by a *lighting director*, who is aided, in turn, by several assistants. EFP shoots are often designed like film productions and thus use many of the same crew members to handle lighting. ENG shoots are often lit solely by the *video producer* or videographer.

THE STUDIO

A sound stage or studio offers the optimum in control for the cinematographer—an enclosed quiet environment with ample electrical power, smooth floors, and high ceilings to accommodate a lighting grid, catwalks, and numerous instruments. The studio allows for the construction of almost any kind of set desired and enables the DP to create practically any style of lighting to suit the mood of the production.

Many American films made prior to the 1960s were primarily studio-shot pictures; lighting style was often dominated by theatrical and formal lighting methods (see any pre-1960 musical for a good example of this). A trend toward realism made extensive location production popular in the 1970s, but extravagant studio filmmaking re-emerged in the 1980s and 1990s with lavish productions like *Pennies from Heaven* (Ross, 1981), *One from the Heart* (Coppola, 1983), *Batman* (Burton, 1989), and *Dick Tracy* (Beatty, 1990).

Lighting style, be it based on high-key, low-key, or modulated value lighting, is best controlled in the studio, which can be any large room or warehouse within which a set can be built. Sets can be constructed to the specifications of the script and the effect desired by the director.

THE TELEVISION STUDIO VS. THE MOTION PICTURE SOUNDSTAGE

A few, fundamental differences exist between the traditional film soundstage and the television studio. The television studio is generally equipped to facilitate several cameras that operate simultaneously via an adjacent control booth. This multicamera mode of production places limits on any lighting plan, as lighting must be general enough to satisfy several points of view at once. Also, television studios are often, by necessity, multiuse facilities. For instance, a television studio may be used to tape a talk show in the morning, an instructional show in the afternoon, and a live audience program in the evening. Since the lighting must be changed quickly for each show, instruments are usually mounted on an overhead grid, which is a lattice of pipe suspended from the ceiling.

Multicamera shoots dictate a more generalized, overall lighting plan, than do single-camera film or EFP shoots, as lighting must be sufficient for all camera vantage points. In general, light stands, which tend to clutter the floor and inhibit the mobility of cameras, are eschewed in favor of scissor-type, extendable *pantographs*, which allow instruments to be brought down close to the subject and moved quickly out of the way when not needed. Scoops are often used to provide an overall fill, known as base light, in order to provide a minimum footcandle level. Lighting plans are plotted for each show so that each lighting scheme may be restored prior to taping a given program.

The motion picture studio or soundstage is usually host to one production at a time, although very large buildings may house several sets in different areas simultaneously. The building may be an actual designated studio building or simply a large, rented warehouse. Often, catwalks (narrow walkways high above and circumscribing the floor area) allow technicians ready access to fixtures without the need to intrude upon sets. Light stands are used frequently. On many soundstages, fixtures are simply mounted high on stands behind flats or affixed directly to the top of set walls. Because each shot is photographed from one camera's point of view,

lighting may be set specifically for virtually any effect desired by the director and cinematographer.

THE CYCLORAMA

In the studio, the cinematographer will sometimes want to idealize and separate a subject from the distractions of a realistic background. A seamless paper or permanent cyclorama backdrop creates a sense of ethereal, limitless space. Highly diffused frontal lighting, used to eliminate shadows and create a very soft gradation of middle tones, completes the illusion. This limbo effect is used frequently by fashion and product photographers as well as videographers and filmmakers.

■ PROJECT 10.1: THE LIMBO EFFECT

Purpose:

To isolate a subject in a featureless environment with wraparound, diffused light.

Materials Needed:

a medium-sized (20 × 30-foot or larger) studio with lighting grid
a continuous tone (all one color) cyclorama or a 9 × 25-foot roll of seamless paper
one to three subjects
video camcorder or camera and VCR
tripod
one 1K focusing spotlight with C-clamp
two broad fixtures with stands
two softlights
two to three sky pans or scoops with C-clamps
toughspun or similar diffusion material
sandbags for stands
three grounded, AC extension cables
black wrap
accessories as needed (gaffer tape, gels, clothespins, etc.)

Procedure:

1. This project is best done in a large studio, but any good-size room with high ceilings will work. If the studio is not equipped with a clean cyc, a seamless paper is also excellent for the limbo effect and is available at *professional* photography dealers. A special frame for holding the paper roll is available, but you can also hang the roll on a telescoping wall spreader bar, such as a pole cat.
2. Unroll the paper down onto the floor and pull it until about 5 feet of the paper rests on the floor. The paper should form a gentle curve as it unrolls.
3. Tape the end of the paper down on the studio floor; make sure you do not crease or indent it and also watch out for shoe scuff marks and footprints. Voila—an instant cyclorama.
4. Hang two to three sky pans or scoops along the top of the cyc so that they illuminate it smoothly (see Figure 10.1). Balance out the lighting with a broad fixture placed on the floor at each side.

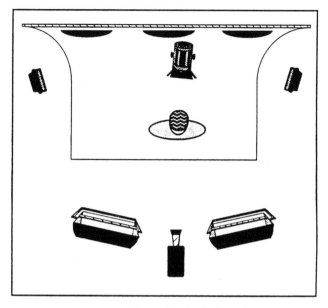

FIGURE 10.1 Lighting for the limbo effect.

5. Block the subject and focus a 1K Fresnel or ellipsoidal fixture, for each figure, to serve as a hair light. You may wish to add a scrim or use a smaller fixture if you desire a more subtle effect. Use a floor-mounted softlight or two to add the necessary frontal fill lighting to complete the effect.

DAY INTERIORS

The first step to designing a convincing lighting style is to decide upon the supposed time of day. This determination will dictate the amount and quality of the illumination, as well as the direction from which the light will emanate. The most logical sources for day interiors are windows. In this case, any practical lamps in the room will be secondary sources. When windows are key sources, the time of day determines whether the light will be directional or diffused, directional lighting.

During most of the day, the sun is so high in the sky that its direct rays stream through windows at sharp angles, casting pools of light only on floors or low portions of walls. A look at most filmed interior scenes of kitchens, living rooms, and bedrooms, however, will reveal shadows of window frames, miniblinds, and shimmering foilage cast distinctly on set walls at all times of the day. In the real world, such shadows occur only in the few hours after the sun rises or before it sets (when it is low enough to actually shine into a window at the proper angle to cast a visible pattern on a wall). At all other times of day, windows are diffused, directional light sources that illuminate objects in smooth, gradated tonalities. Nevertheless, interiors with windows are almost always shot to look like early morning or late afternoon, as the shadows created by the raking sunlight are much more interesting than flat fields of diffused light on subjects and backgrounds.

LIGHTING DESIGNS

The following pages contain several advanced lighting projects, each of which uses a different lighting approach for selected daytime interiors to be shot in a studio. Since available studio space and the numbers and types of available lighting instruments may vary, these lighting designs are suggested as starting points for creating various scenes.

In order to duplicate these setups, you will need the following:

a studio or similar large interior space
a set
at least three focusing spots or other directional fixtures
at least two softlights or bounce lights
several broads, nooks, or similar background lights
C-stands
various barndoors, scrims, nets, and flags

■ PROJECT 10.2: HIGH-KEY LIVING ROOM—AFTERNOON

If a set is constructed to the director's specifications and a living room interior is desired, the walls will generally include one or more large windows revealing a view of the outside (see Figure 10.2). In the studio, a realistic backdrop (a painted, flat, or commercially available panorama) of an exterior scene is positioned several feet beyond any windows that will appear in the scene. Light the backdrop with sky pans, striplights, or any open-faced instruments that may be placed along the top of the flat (a panel representing a set wall). The object is to illuminate the background as evenly as possible in order to preserve the illusion of a window view. Large Fresnel fixtures placed near the top of the flat to flood the room with light will produce a sunny effect. Additional broads at the outside edges of the window will add to the effect of streaming sunlight. An arc, HMI, or other large fixture may be placed outside the window to create distinct shadows cast from window sash frames or blinds.

Set the blocking (areas that the actors will occupy through the duration of the take). Set key lights to cover the action. This may take the form of a generalized key lighting scheme, if the actors move freely around the room. If the actors are seated or the action is localized, then it may be possible to set a single key light for a more dramatic effect. Again, windows are the most logical and convincing sources for determining light motivation and direction.

Turn on any practical lamps you wish to appear in the set; focus spotlights on the walls and furniture around the practicals to give the look of natural lamp spill light. Be careful not to cast obvious shadows from the fixtures. With the actors or stand-ins in their places, you may now add kicker or back light. If you desire a more realistic style, you may decide to forego all unmotivated light entirely. The final step is to set one or two fill lights near the camera and bring the shadow area to the proper lighting ratio.

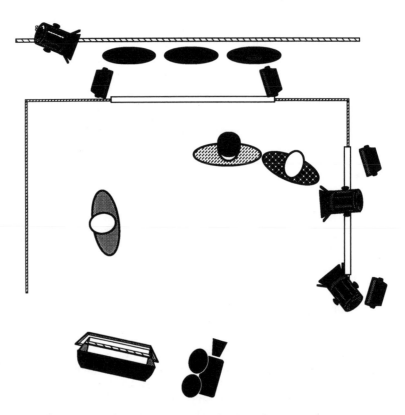

FIGURE 10.2 High-key living room.

■ PROJECT 10.3: BEDROOM SIDE LIGHTING—EARLY MORNING

Crisp morning sunlight streaming through a bedroom window is a pleasing effect that is easily achieved with strong side lighting. This project uses the Hopper-style lighting discussed in Chapter Nine.

For this full shot, the key light (a 2K or 5K spot) is positioned (to illuminate the subject) approximately 90° from the subject's side (opposite the camera) at close to the standing eye level (see Figure 10.3 and Figure 9.2). Only one side of the subject's face is illuminated. The other side is left in shadow and is lit only when the actor turns into the light. Depending on the mood desired, the lighting ratio can be lessened by rigging softlights overhead.

A diffused key, such as a softlight, is used in the close-ups, and the key may be brought in closer than the full-shot key. A 5K Fresnel is ideal for simulating sunlight in the full shot, but a smaller tungsten fixture, such as a 1K baby, will put out much more light if the lens is removed, albeit with some loss of modeling control (*do not* operate an arc or HMI without its lens).

Amber gels on the motivating key will warm the key light to resemble the honey-colored glow of early morning sun. Smoke or aerosol diffusion will also enhance the particulate look of sun rays streaming in the window.

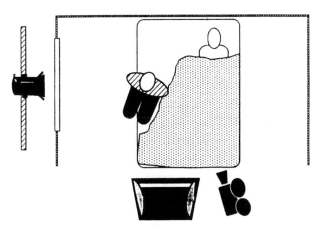

FIGURE 10.3 Bedroom side lighting.

NIGHT INTERIORS

■ PROJECT 10.4: THE NIGHT OFFICE

In this night scene of a figure seated in a small office, a single, bare light bulb hanging from a cord becomes the motivating source (see Figure 10.4). The glaring surface of the light bulb may be dimmed by applying a light coating of brown haircolor spray (such as Streaks-n-Tips). A focusing spot can be keyed on the figure to imitate the hanging lamp. Allow the figure to lean in to the glare of the lamp for added realism.

Outside the window, a flashing red-gelled key effects light will give the impression of a neon sign just outside the window. A blue-gelled kicker will suggest the glow of night.

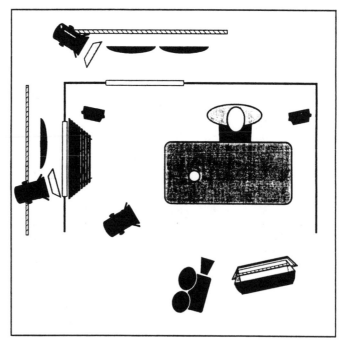

FIGURE 10.4 Low-key office at night.

Close-ups in a low-key scene usually require a lower lighting ratio to bring up shadow detail in the face. This effect is accomplished by using a carefully controlled bounce light for a ratio of 6:1.

■ PROJECT 10.5: LIVING ROOM CROSS-KEY LIGHTING—EVENING

In evening scenes, practical lamps become the natural point of motivation. The available illumination of any practicals can be increased by replacing standard incandescent bulbs with high-output photofloods, thus raising the color temperature and the luminous intensity of the fixtures. The light from such a motivated source does not provide enough illumination in itself to act as a key, but can fill areas in a background and boost overall base light.

The familiar, hourglass-shaped pattern formed by the light spilling from the top and bottom of a practical's lampshade should not be more than 2 stops brighter than the key-lit action. Some light may also emanate from a moonlit window or fireplace (see Figure 10.5). If a fire is burning in the hearth, it can be a motivational source. If the fireplace is not seen from the front in a given shot, spots may be placed inside the fireplace to serve as key lights in the scene. When the fireplace appears in the shot, focusing spotlights should be placed as close as possible to the hearth without becoming noticeable. For close-ups, the instruments may be angled up from low angles and their beams shielded by flags so they do not flare in the camera lens.

At some angles, the fireplace key lights will be behind the actors and thus act as kickers. In this case, place two additional keys on each side, goboing them to illuminate only the faces and fronts of the subjects. The crossed keys will light the front of one actor and provide hair light to the other actor at the same time. Unless a low-key effect is desired, the entire face should not be in shadow. One more barndoor spot, positioned on one side and focused softly on the fireplace, will bring out texture, but should be kept 2 stops below the total exposure level.

The top and sides of the frame may be allowed to go dark, depending on the desired mood. Any practicals in the scene may be turned on and spotted from above. Add fill light to bring up the lighting ratio to a 6:1 or 4:1 ratio.

In a low-key lighting setup, the key light must be meticulously set to limit its illumination to the subject only. It is help-

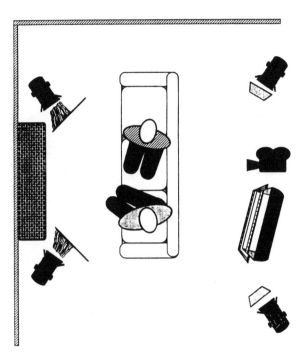

FIGURE 10.5   Evening living room cross-key lighting. Flicker sticks (described in Project 10.6) simulate flames burning in the fireplace.

ful to consider the set in three planes—background, foreground, and action area—each of which should be lit separately. Lights in a low-key configuration should not overlap, at the risk of destroying the air of intrigue usually desired in such a style.

Place the keys between the actor and the background, and as close to the ceiling as possible parallel to the direction of action. Angle the keys to light the short side of the subject's face (opposite the camera), so that the cheek patch of light falls on the shaded side of the face. Narrow the vertical blades of the barndoor to cut any spill light. Adjust the background illumination until it is at least 2 stops under the key illumination.

NIGHT EXTERIORS

Daytime exterior shots in studios generally require extensive sets and backgrounds to produce a convincing rendition of reality. Even daytime exterior shots as elaborate as Alfred Hitchcock's (e.g., *Rear Window*) look fake by today's standards, because multiple source studio lighting simply does not look like daylight. Because multiple light sources occur naturally outside at night, it is often easier to simulate night exteriors in a studio than one might guess. They can be shot in a stylized way (*One from the Heart* [Coppola, 1981], *Batman* [Burton, 1989]) or in a more realistic fashion (*Home Alone* [Columbus, 1990]). Night scenes in *Close Encounters of the Third Kind* (Spielberg, 1977) were shot on a huge soundstage that housed an entire farmhouse. The following project is a simpler night scene that produces excellent results with modest facilities and equipment.

■ PROJECT 10.6: MOONLIT NIGHT BY A CAMPFIRE

When shooting exteriors in a studio, the most important element for achieving any degree of realism is the backdrop. Scenery backdrops are commercially available, but can also be painted on large canvases called *flats*. A painted backdrop of a beach, ocean view, or mountains with trees can enhance the scene of a group gathered around a campfire. For this night scene, however, a black curtain or backdrop is enough to make the background a dark void.

It is not necessary to have an actual fire on the set—an establishing shot (a shot that identifies locale) can be taken at an actual outdoor site under *available* (read *no additional*) lighting and used to recreate a simulated scene. Block the actors in a circle around the supposed fire, at least 10 feet from the backdrop. Place the camera back far enough from the action and use a longer lens to decrease the depth of field and further separate the characters from their surroundings. Rig a 2K or 5K Fresnel (HMIs are ideal) high, behind, and to the side as far back as possible; this is the kicker. Gel the kicker with blue (unless it is an HMI) to simulate the full moon.

The fire is the motivating source, so use it as a clue for setting the keys. Place two babies low, in front, and on either side of the ring (see Figure 10.6). A rod or dowel hung with strips of orange, red, yellow, and an odd-green gel can be waved in front of the babies; this *flicker stick* (see Figure 10.7) mimics the undulating glimmer of actual flames.

If less contrast is desired for close-ups, a gelled softlight fill can be added, along with smoke from a fog machine to complete the scene.

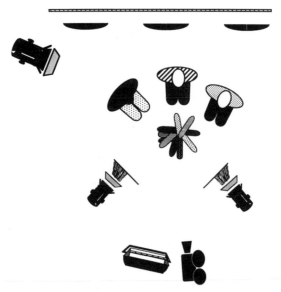

FIGURE 10.6 Moonlit night by a campfire.

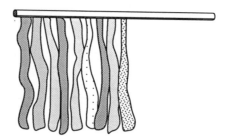

FIGURE 10.7 A flicker stick, which is used for simulating firelight.

KEY for LIGHTING PLOTS

Lowell Tota-light

200w Pepper

1K Fresnel

2K Fresnel

5K Fresnel

Skypan

Broad or Nook

Softlight

Pro-light

650w Compact

Video Camera

Film Camera

Subjects

Scrim

Gel

Flicker Stick

Butterfly/Silk

Cookie

Shiny Board

Foam Core or Show Card

Flag

CHAPTER ELEVEN

Lighting on Location

INTRODUCTION

Location shoots (known as *remote production* in video) have been an important part of production since early in this century when independent film companies left the eastern United States for the year-round, sunny climate of southern California. Location production, which includes all shooting that does not take place in a studio, can yield more realistic and convincing footage. Location production does not, however, give the cinematographer the control of the studio. Thus, careful planning is critical.

LOCATION SCOUTING AND PLANNING

Go to the location well before the shoot and note the physical features of the location, including the size and shape of the room, the height of the ceiling, the availability of power, and the configuration of the circuits. Make sure that power and ventilation are not shut off during the time scheduled for the shoot. Decide on the number and type of instruments required for the shoot and the method of mounting them. The director who fails to review the location before the day production begins risks embarrassing surprises when the crew arrives.

Some important steps for previewing a location are:

1. Note the dimensions of the area or room.
2. Sketch out lighting positions, camera angles, and blocking of the actors.
3. Determine your power requirements and available amperage at the location.
4. Decide what special lighting requirements are necessary.

DAY EXTERIORS

The French Impressionist painter Claude Monet demonstrated the effects of continually changing sunlight in a series of canvases depicting the cathedral at Rouen during different times of the day. These paintings demonstrated how harsh midday light contrasted dramatically with late afternoon rays that raked across the cathedral's facade, defining its myriad details and textures.

The cinematographer will also learn much about a desired location by observing and photographing the location at various times of day. A Polaroid or standard 35mm camera is handy for taking snapshots as visual records of the site. A hand-held compass helps to judge and predict sunlight positions for different hours of the day. Determine which side of a street will receive full sun, partial shade, or full shadow at any given time—you will have an accurate picture of the conditions at the time of the shooting.

Block scenes so that the shadows are consistent with shot continuity. If the master scene is shot during the morning hours and the close-ups shot later in the afternoon, be sure to cheat the actors' positions so that shadow directions and backgrounds in the scenes match. This is particularly crucial if *pickups* (shoots deemed necessary to preserve continuity, often shot several days or weeks after principal photography) are needed later.

The aim of most exterior lighting is to reduce the harsh contrast of sunlight, which exceeds the contrast range of film and video. Direct sunlight is often filtered by means of a butterfly or an overhead. In many cases, the sun becomes a backlight or kicker, with supplemental fill light provided by carbon arcs, HMIs, PAR-FAY clusters, or reflectors.

When windy locations or enclosed areas make lighting with reflectors impractical, artificial sources must be used. The problem is that any artificial source must be of sufficient intensity in order to fill in the deep shadows cast by the sun. Therefore, conventional tungsten sources (which must be filtered with blue gels to match daylight) are not particularly useful under these circumstances. Only high-intensity, daylight-balanced sources, such as carbon arcs, HMIs, and PAR-FAYs, are practical for use in daylight. Such high-intensity lamps draw a great deal of current (as much as 225 amps for brutes) and require the use of a high-power generator.

■ PROJECT 11.1: LIGHTING A DAYLIGHT EXTERIOR

Purpose:

To use reflectors and diffusion materials to reduce contrast in an outdoor one shot.

Materials Needed:

model
partly shaded courtyard or similar location
camera and tripod
two C-stands
shiny board and stand
4 × 4-foot butterfly
two 20 × 30-inch foam core sheets, 48 × 60-inch showcards, or stretched Griffolyn sheets
sandbags

When shooting a medium one shot or two-shot on a sunny day, you have the option of placing the subject in either a sunlit or shady area. Direct sun has the disadvantage of high contrast—harsh highlights and dark shadows. The sun's continuous movement also causes problems of changing light direction that can be quite drastic through the course of several takes. Selecting a shady area is not without its problems as well, as background area may be unacceptably bright, ambient reflected light from pavement or foliage may be difficult to control, and the subject itself may appear to be quite flat.

An effective alternative is to use shade augmented with extra light. The most controllable method of adding daylight-balanced light is with HMI or FAY lights, which have the high intensity needed to fill in sun-cast shadows. Since the cost and power requirements of such fixtures are beyond the budget of all but big production companies, the next best choice involves using filtered sunlight filled in with reflectors.

Procedure:

1. Place the subject at the edge of a shaded area in a courtyard with the camera and tripod set up approximately 8 feet away. At this point, at midmorning, the key light cast by the sun on the short side of the subject's face is overly bright and harsh; meanwhile, the dark foliage and shrubbery in the background appears too dark. Therefore, shape the existing light to create an aesthetically pleasing shot (see Figure 11.1).
2. Mount a 4 × 4-foot silk or lavender butterfly on a high roller stand and adjust it to take the edge off specular sunlight on the subject.
3. With the key light brought down to a manageable level, bring up the lighting ratio through the use of reflectors.
4. Now bring up the background foliage by setting up a high riser stand and reflector board to the camera's left. Focus the soft side of the board on the greenery to bring out the overall detail. The soft side will provide a larger illuminated surface than the highly specular hard side, which may create a hot spot on the foliage. If necessary, dim the reflector board with a slip-on net.
5. Lighten the shaded broad side of the subject's face with a white reflector, such as a foam core panel of a Griffolyn sheet stretched on a frame. Mount the white reflector on a C-stand 4 feet from the subject and just off the left border of the frame. The reflected light from a white sheet falls off dramatically as its distance from the subject becomes greater, so it is easy to change the fill level dramatically simply by moving the reflector. Since some cameras take in slightly more picture area than their viewfinders indicate, it is wise to keep all reflectors and lights well out of frame.

With a minimum of equipment, this lighting setup takes little time, keeps the subject comfortable, and produces high-quality results. Though all situations present different requirements, most problems encountered with this or a similar setup may be overcome by experimenting with different types of nets, scrims, diffusions, reflectors, and reflective surfaces.

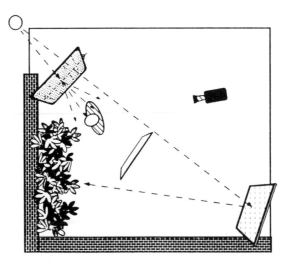

FIGURE 11.1 Lighting a daylight exterior.

NIGHT EXTERIORS

Night shoots present special problems for the cinematographer. At night, it is one thing to light a city street scene or a suburban house exterior, and quite another when the shoot is to take place in the great outdoors away from towns, buildings, and motivating light sources such as streetlights. The cinematographer has a choice of shooting night with available light, shooting at night with studio lights, or shooting day-for-night.

Day-for-Night

Day-for-night, which entails faking a night look in a scene while shooting during daylight hours, has fallen out of favor as film and television audiences have become more visually aware. There are few viable alternatives, however, when budgets are low or when the shoot must take place in remote, natural surroundings. Day-for-night, therefore, remains one of the most effective ways to capture a night effect in the open country.

Compared with actual night shooting, day-for-night is a relatively simple procedure. The primary objective is to impart a convincing moonlit appearance. Thus, it is best to shoot in the early morning or late afternoon when the sun achieves its greatest angle and shadows cast by the sun are long. Shadows can be further enhanced by blocking action so that light comes from a kicker position, about 130° off the camera axis.

An ND.6 filter will allow for a wider aperture and will decrease the depth of field; a polarizer or graduate will darken the sky for static camera setups. Even so, it is wise to include as little sky as possible, as any clouds will give away the day-for-night effect. A "midnight cast" may be added by using a blue filter or by leaving off the #85 B (or replacing it with a #81 EF), if shooting tungsten film. A #23 red filter for sky darkening, combined with a #56 green to ensure good flesh tones, is a traditional combination for black-and-white cinematography.

Day-for-night is often most effective when shot during the "magic hour"—the period of dusk just after the sun sets. The major problem with this approach is the short time available for shooting, magic hour usually lasts no more than 20 minutes. Day-for-night scenes are even more realistic when nighttime lights, including automobile headlamps, streetlights, and lighted windows, are illuminated to appear in the shot. For a breathtaking example of a film shot entirely on location, much of it using available light during magic hour, see *Days of Heaven* (Malick, 1977), which won DPs Nestor Almendros and Haskell Wexler an Academy Award for cinematography.

Night-for-Night

The most convincing night photography is indeed shot at night. This is particularly true when scenes take place in urban or suburban areas where ambient illumination emanates from streetlights, building lamps, signs, and automobile headlights.

Using Ambient Sources

The cinematographer will sometimes need to shoot a night scene using practical sources alone. It is frequently impossible to access electrical power or take the time required to rig lights in outdoor locations. It is then necessary to use ambient light as a primary source, providing the filmmaker is willing to accept some compromises in picture contrast, shadow detail, and resolution.

Streetlights alone are too high off the ground to cast much

light on a subject. Illuminated signs may be effective depending on the amount of the light they give off, their color, and how close they are to the subject. Building lights (such as porch lights) are useful, as are banks and bulbs, such as those lighting storefronts and movie marquees. The most important factor is always the intensity of the light source.

The more practicals available on a given location, the better for ambient light photography. If possible, replace existing standard tungsten lamps with the highest watt photoflood lamps that the socket can handle. (Many sockets have labels that warn against using anything higher than a 100-watt lamp to avoid overloads.) If practicals cannot be replaced, other methods may be necessary to use them as keys.

Night-for-night shooting often requires particular light sources that must be specially constructed or rigged. A practical such as a hanging porch fixture, for example, may be augmented by concealing a small, bare, 250- or 500-watt tungsten-halogen lamp (or *peanut*) in or behind the practical. Thus, the light emitted by the peanut should appear to be emanating from the practical itself. The simplest way to hide a peanut is to hide it inside the shade behind the actual practical lamp, wrapping the wiring of the peanut around the cord of the existing fixture. The peanut must not touch anything surrounding the fixture; it should also have sufficient ventilation.

As we saw in Chapter Five, varying color temperatures in practical sources present real problems to the cinematographer. A continuing trend toward greater realism in night cinematography has made the odd-colored glow of industrial lamps more acceptable as practicals on the periphery of the scene. The presence of orange incandescents, green fluorescents, greenish blue mercury vapors, and amber and pink sodiums make color balancing a challenging experience.

High-contrast lighting, to be avoided in many exterior daylight situations, enhances the authenticity of exterior night scenes. Contrast, which serves to separate subjects from the background, is enhanced further by strong side lighting. Side light from streetlights provides the motivation for the lighting in the following project.

■ PROJECT 11.2: NIGHT EXTERIOR—SIDEWALK ON A RESIDENTIAL STREET

Purpose:

To simulate ambient light in a typical night exterior.

Materials Needed:

two subjects
video camcorder or camera and VCR
tripod
incident meter for determining light ratios
two or more 1K Fresnel spots, mickeys, or PAR cans
one 2K Fresnel
generator or other 110-volt AC source
blue, amber, and yellow gels
three full scrims or nets
three half scrims
at least two sandbags per light stand
at least six 50-foot grounded, AC extension cables
black wrap
accessories as needed (gaffer tape, gels, clothespins, etc.)

Procedure:

1. This scene includes a couple walking down a quiet, suburban sidewalk at night. Take your motivation cues from street lamps or other regularly spaced fixtures that occur naturally in the area, such as building lights. Set a 1K spot at 10–15-feet intervals; you may want to gel the spots with amber or yellow to imitate the odd light of sodium or mercury vapor lamps (see Figure 11.2).

2. If the shot takes place in a more urban environment, take your cue from the closest ambient sources—neon lights or the fluorescents in storefront windows (in the case of the latter, large-area sources like softlights may better simulate the supposed window light).

3. Mount a blue-gelled 2K or larger spot on a high riser to give a moonlight or streetlight kick. Remember to use one sandbag for every riser column you extend.

4. If you can plug into the power of a nearby house, do so; if the source is too far away, however, you will suffer a drop in voltage (which means dimmer and yellower light). Use 10- or 12-gauge cables of 100 feet or less. If AC power is unavailable or you are using HMIs, you will have to have a generator that can produce at least 40 amps.

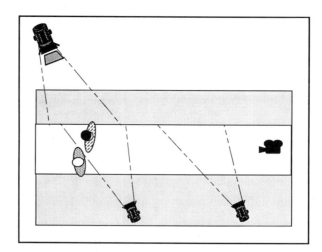

FIGURE 11.2   Night exterior—a sidewalk stroll.

DAY INTERIORS

Location daytime interiors are generally illuminated by window light and may be lit using variations on the basic motivated, window lighting plans found in Chapter Nine. The problem with window light on sunny days is that light constantly changes throughout the course of the day. What we barely perceive becomes quite apparent as scenes with windows are filmed over several hours. The continuity problems posed by sunny windows can be very distracting, as shadows and hot spots change radically from full shot to medium shot. The best course of action is to avoid sunny windows as much as possible and shoot them when they are in shade. If a sunlight effect is essential, a shady window lit by an HMI or arc lamp just outside the window can provide such an effect.

Most modern offices and other places of business are lit primarily with banks of overhead fluorescent light and many of these same settings are also replete with large windows. The most convincing approach for shooting in such a situation is to go with the dominant motivating source—usually the fluorescents if the windows are heavily tinted. The following project is one solution to lighting the daytime office problem.

■ PROJECT 11.3:   BALANCING SOURCES IN A DAYTIME OFFICE

Purpose:

To light a daytime location interior with augmented available light.

Materials Needed:

a medium-to-large-size room
fluorescent and window light
desk
chairs
one subject
video camcorder or camera and VCR
tripod
incident meter for determining light ratios
one teenie
one scissor clamp
two 1K Nooklights or broads
one softlight
three full scrims or nets
three half scrims
two sandbags
at least four 25-foot grounded, AC extension cables
a large roll of Tough Plusgreen/Windowgreen
Tough Plusgreen 50 for fixtures
black wrap
accessories as needed (gaffer tape, clothespins, etc.)

Procedure:

Figure 11.3 represents a typical modern office, replete with large, tinted windows and overhead fluorescent lighting.
If you augment this available light with tungsten instruments, you will be faced with three different color temperatures.

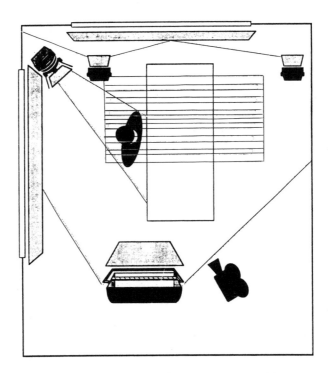

FIGURE 11.3. A daytime office location lit with gelled window light, overhead fluorescents, and gelled tungsten.

1. Determine the dominant light source. During the day, most interiors with large windows are lit primarily by sun and skylight. In many modern office buildings, however, the large windows are heavily tinted, making the fluorescents the primary source. Hence, for shooting convincing realistic office scenes, it is best to use the ambient fluorescents as a main source and filter your other sources to match it. This means gelling windows with Tough Plusgreen/Windowgreen and gelling tungsten sources with Tough Plusgreen 50.
2. Attach the large sheet gels to the windows by taping the gel perimeter to the window frame. Make sure that any seams are not noticeable on camera.
3. White balance the video camera for the prevailing fluorescent green light. If you are using film, use a daylight-balanced emulsion and filter the lens with a CCM30 lens filter as well. If you are using many tungsten sources and few fluorescents, leave the tungsten unfiltered and filter the fluorescents with fluorofilter sheets; use CTO gel on any windows.
4. After gelling the windows, hang a teenie or pepper as a backlight high behind the seated subject by means of a scissor clamp rigged to the dropped ceiling. If the background walls need bringing up, hide a nook or small broad in the corners—be careful, however, not to make walls unnaturally hot.
5. Set a softlight near the camera to fill in the harsh fluorescent light.

PRE-RIGGING

Prerigging means rigging your lights before the shooting day or at least well before the rest of the crew arrives. Determine the amperage of circuits and note how they are distributed throughout the building you will be using. Lay and tape down enough AC cable to power all lights needed to illuminate the sets. By all means, try to mount the instruments above the set with as few floor stands as possible. Light stands clutter the set, intrude on the action, and invite accidents. Often, lightweight instruments can be clamped to rafters, moldings, or doors and doorway lintels. In rooms with dropped ceilings, it is possible to use special scissor clamps to hang light fixtures from the T-bar, dropped ceiling frame. Since many actual locations do not offer overhead mounting possibilities, however, it is usually necessary to rig some kind of overhead grid.

The Location Lighting Grid

The small rooms and cramped spaces common to many location interiors often prohibit the use of light stands. Light stands also intrude on camera framing, particularly with moving camera shots. A grid is indispensable in this instance. A grid is simply a pipe or several pipes fastened together and suspended from the ceiling above a set to support lighting fixtures. The grid can be as modest as a single furniture clamp, similar to a woodworking bar clamp, which is used to span

doorways, rafters, and ceiling vaults. Instruments may be attached quickly with C-clamps. A fixture may also be affixed directly to walls or ceilings with a baby plate, a plate with a 5/8-inch pin for mounting lightweight lighting instruments that can be nailed or taped to a surface. Pole cats, spring-loaded telescoping poles that are mounted vertically in out-of-the-way areas, are another convenient way to mount lights in a limited space. A more elaborate grid may be constructed from aluminum conduit or from 2 × 3-foot fir studs in 8-foot lengths suspended near the ceiling. With the grid in place, fixtures may be rigged high enough to allow complete freedom of both actor and camera movement.

Lighting a Controlled Group

Everyone is familiar with Leonardo da Vinci's painting, *The Last Supper*, which depicts Christ and his apostles seated along one side of a long table. The power of this fresco is the frankly theatrical composition, which reveals the expressions of all 13 apostles at the moment Christ tells of his eventual betrayal by one of them. Bold as it is, this blocking would not work in a realistic scene, because people almost never all sit on one side of a table. Lighting a number of seated figures facing one another in a natural manner is a problem that calls for a somewhat different approach than Leonardo's *bas-relief* style. The following project is one solution to lighting a group gathered around a table.

■ PROJECT 11.4: LIGHTING A CONTROLLED GROUP (TABLE)

Purpose:

To light a seated group with a minimum of equipment.

Materials Needed:

a medium-size room
table and chairs
three to five subjects
video camcorder or camera and VCR
tripod
incident meter for determining light ratios
two 1K mickeys or 650W teenies
two 1K Nooklights or broads
three 200W peppers
two softlights
three full scrims or nets
three half scrims
three ¼ scrims, if available
two sandbags
at least eight 25-foot grounded, AC extension cables
black wrap
accessories as needed (gaffer tape, gels, clothespins, etc.)

Procedure:

1. This project involves a discussion scene with four or five actors seated around a dinner table. Block the actors around the table as shown in Figure 11.4. Most tables are illuminated by an overhead fixture, so this will provide the motivation for this lighting plan.
2. An overhead source alone can create unwanted facial shadows and harsh hot light on the tops of heads, so use the grid to hand additional instruments to create key, back, and fill light. A scene such as this will be more pleasing if the walls are painted a medium-dark color, rather than white.

FIGURE 11.4 Lighting grid plan for a group seated around a table.

3. Rig a grid using telescoping wall spreaders that are secured high above the table. Make sure they span the room's shorter dimension.

4. Be sure not to overload any one circuit; run extension cords to various circuits throughout the house and tape down cables to keep them out of the way.

5. Hang a large softlight directly over the table.

6. Rig a 1K mickey or 650W teenie as a key on either side of the table, high and behind each row of diners.

7. Use a half or quarter scrim in each to eliminate hot spots on the table.

8. Hang two broads to illuminate the back wall. You may wish to use a half or quarter scrim on each to even out the distribution of the light.

9. Add separation with three high, small spots (peppers, inkies, or tweenies) and perhaps amber or blue gel to add effect. You might decide to add an extra softlight in front of the scene, if a flatter light is desired.

LIGHTING IN THE REAL WORLD

As you try these setups, you will undoubtedly find that lighting for film and video is a time-intensive business. Now is the time to experiment; try different approaches to orthodox lighting situations; learn rules and then break them. The great cinematographers have all parted with tradition to advance the art. Vilmos Zsigmond pushed and flashed film beyond some industry people's belief on Robert Altman's pictures, Vittorio Storaro gelled his lights to screaming primary hue saturation levels in *One from the Heart*, Nestor Almendros eschewed the use of Fresnels entirely on more than one motion picture, and Gordon Willis deliberately lit the *Godfather* films to leave actors' eyes in deep shadow. By all means, break rules—but learn them first.

In the real world of production, time is money and much pressure is put on the photography unit to proceed as swiftly as possible. It may become difficult to be creative and maintain high lighting standards if the production unit is under the gun to shoot 7–10 pages of script a day. Nonetheless, everyone from the director to the lowliest group will agree that a carefully lit film is well worth the pains taken to create it. The satisfaction of doing one's very best and seeing the result of the contribution is the greatest payoff of all.

Filters for Light Balancing and Color Compensating

Product No.	Name	Description	Mired Shift Value	Transmission
Filters for Light Balancing (LB); Kelvin Adjustment				
Amber Filters to Reduce Kelvin				
		The standard filter to convert		
3401	RoscoSun 85	5500°K daylight to a nominal 3200°K	+131	58%
3407	RoscoSun CTO*	5500°K daylight to a nominal 2900°K	+167	47%
3408	RoscoSun 1/2 CTO*	5500°K daylight to a nominal 3800°K	+81	73%
3409	RoscoSun 1/4 CTO*	5500°K daylight to a nominal 4500°K	+42	81%
3410	RoscoSun 1/8 CTO*	5500°K daylight to a nominal 4900°K	+20	92%
Blue Filters to Increase Kelvin				
		The standard filter to convert		
3202	Full Blue (Tough Blue 50)	3200°K to a nominal 5500°K daylight	−131	36%
3204	Half Blue (Tough Booster Blue)**	3200°K to a nominal 4100°K	−68	52%
3206	Third Blue (Tough 1/2 Booster Blue)**	3200°K to a nominal 3800°K	−49	64%
3208	Quarter Blue (Tough 1/4 Booster Blue)**	3200°K to a nominal 3500°K	−30	74%
3216	Eighth Blue (Tough 1/8 Booster Blue)**	3200°K to a nominal 3300°K	−12	81%
Combination Filters to Deal with Green Content and Kelvin				
3310	Fluorofilter	Reduces green and corrects cool white fluorescents to a nominal 3200°K	N/A	36%
3306	Tough Plusgreen 50	Increases green and corrects 3200°K sources to nominally balance to cool white fluorescents	N/A	45%

Product No.	Name	Nominal CC Equivalent	For Use When Indicated CC Index Is Approximately	Transmission
Filters for Color Compensating (CC); Green Adjustment				
*Green Filters to Reduce Magenta Content***				
3304	Tough Plusgreen	30	−12	76%
3315	Tough 1/2 Plusgreen	15	−5	90%

97

Product No.	Name	Nominal CC Equivalent	For Use When Indicated CC Index Is Approximately	Transmission
3316	Tough 1/4 Plusgreen	75	−2	92%
Magenta Filters to Reduce Green Content				
3308	Tough Minusgreen	30	+13	55%
3313	Tough 1/2 Minusgreen	15	+6	71%
3314	Tough 1/4 Minusgreen	75	+3	81%

*Reduces to Kelvin temperature output of any source (see mired shift value). We use 5500°K here as a reference.

**Increases Kelvin temperature output of any source (see mired shift value), including HMI, CID, etc. We use 3200°K here as a reference.

***These series of green, magenta, and combination filters are used to increase or reduce the green component when balancing fluorescent and discharge lamps to each other, to tungsten, or to daylight.

Courtesy of Rosco Laboratories, Inc.

Some Additional Rosco Filters for Special Applications

Product No.	Name	Description	Mired Shift Value	Transmission
3107	Tough Y1	Pale straw filter frequently used in the US to inhabit UV transmission and slightly warm daylight balance arcs.	+45	93%
3110	Tough WF Green	Preferred in European applications for the same purpose as Y1.	+20	86%
3102	Tough MT2	Often used as an amber conversion for arcs and HMI lights. Used in combination with Y1 for correcting 5500°K white flame arcs and HMI lights to 3200°K.	+110	66%
3106	Tough MTY	A single filter combining MT2 and Y1 for correction of 5500°K white flame arcs and HMI to 3200°K.	+131	57%
3114	Tough UV Filter	Virtually clear filters that absorb 90% of UV wavelengths below 390 nanometers. Eliminates fluorescing effect of UV-rich sources in whites. Subtle amber cast warms light slightly.	+8	93%
3115	Tough 1/2 MT2	Partial amber correction, nominally half that of MT2, often used on white flame arcs and HMI.	+38	84%
3116	Tough 1/4 MT2	Partial amber correction, nominally one-quarter that of MT2, often used on white flame arcs and HMI.	+20	91%
3134	Tough MT54	Straw correction for white flame arcs, HMI, or other applications where a gentle warming is required.	+35	83%
3402	RoscoSun N3	Neutral density filter often used on window to reduce the level of incident daylight. Reduces light intensity 1 stop.	N/A	50%
3403	RoscoSun N6	Reduces light intensity 2 stops.	N/A	25%

Product No.	Name	Description	Mired Shift Value	Transmission
3404	RoscoSun N9	Reduces light intensity 3 stops.	N/A	12%
8073	Polarizing Filter	A special effect filter to reduce glare. This linear polarizing filter is available in 19-in × 20-in (48cm × 51cm) sheets.	N/A	38%

Courtesy of Rosco Laboratories, Inc.

GLOSSARY

acetate a clear sheet plastic, cellulose triacetate, used as a base for motion picture film and filter gels

additive process a system of color photography that adds together lights of the three additive primary colors—red, green, and blue—in different degrees to form an image; the additive process is no longer used in cinematography, although a form of it is still employed in video imaging

aerosol diffusion an aerosol spray used to create a fog or smoke effect

alternating current (AC) electrical current that reverses directional flow at regular intervals; in the United States, electrical current supplied by power companies alternates at a rate of 60 Hertz

ambient light naturally occuring available light

ampere or amp a basic unit of electrical current (amps = watts/volts)

aperture the adjustable opening of a camera iris that passes light in controlled intensities; the size of a given aperture determines its f-stop

apple box an enclosed, sturdy wooden box with a grip hole in either end; used as a small platform for elevating props and equipment, for leveling uneven surfaces, and for standing or sitting; four commonly used sizes—full apple (12 in × 8 in × 20 in), half apple (12 in × 4 in × 20 in), quarter apple (12 in × 2 in × 20 in), and eighth apple or pancake (12 in × 1 in × 20 in)

arc a high-intensity lamp that creates an intense specular light when electrical current sparks continuously between negative and positive rods or electrodes; arc sources may be open-arc, as with the carbon arc lamp, or enclosed-arc, as with the xenon and HMI lamps

art director oversees construction of sets to production designer's specifications; also called set designer

ASA rating a numerical rating of the sensitivity of film emulsion to light as determined by the American Standards Association (now the American National Standards Institute); ASA is a traditional term that has been largely replaced by like terms *exposure index* (EI) and *ISO rating* (combining ASA and European DIN standards)

attenuator a filter that modulates from a specific density to clear glass or acrylic; a graduated filter

automatic exposure a reflective light metering system, used in video and certain still and motion picture cameras that automatically adjusts the iris in response to light levels within the field of view

available light light existing naturally within a given area

baby a focusing Fresnel fixture with a 1000-watt lamp

backdrop a large screen, photographic enlargement, or painted scene used to represent a natural landscape or to create a general limbo effect behind a subject on a studio set

background light illumination directed at a wall or background of a set; used to define the character of the background surface and separate the background from the subject

backlight separates the subject from the background; also called *separation light*; emanates from a source aimed toward the camera lens from above and behind the subject (as a hair light) or behind and to the side (as a kicker); often eschewed by professionals who disdain unmotivated lighting

ballast a device that regulates voltage and serves as a starter in an HMI or other discharge-type lamp; often housed in a separate box that accompanies the fixture

bank a group of lights used to create a larger more powerful light source, such as in a nine-light cluster

barndoor a lighting accessory made up of two or four hinged blades that attach to the front of a lighting fixture; can be rotated and the blades independently adjusted to direct and shape the beam, control spill light, create shadows, and prevent the lamp from flaring in a camera lens

base light overall diffused illumination on a set to ensure an adequate light level for video cameras

bead board polystyrene foam sheeting available in 4 ft × 8 ft × ¾ in sizes; highly porous surface makes it an excellent reflector and a good sound insulator

beam angle the point at which the intensity of a source drops to 50% of maximum (center reading) measured in degrees of the full angle

best boy an electrician who is first assistant to the gaffer

black body a theoretical carbon body that has 0% reflectance; used as a standard to determine color temperature of radiating sources in degrees Kelvin

black wrap a heavyweight, flexible, matte black material used for improvising gobos and snoots; used as a heat shield between a hot fixture and a heat-sensitive surface

blade a narrow flag

blocking staging the actors on a set in relation to the camera

boiloff the tendency of standard incandescent lamps to disperse molecules of tungsten from the filament to the inside of the envelope; continues with lamp use and results in a steadily deteriorating filament and a gradual darkening of the light bulb

boomerang a receptacle in front of a fixture that holds filters

booster blue a #80A filter used to boost the color temperature of tungsten lamps from 3200°K to 5500°K

bounce lighting a large diffused source created by reflecting light off white-colored or neutral-colored surfaces such as ceilings, wall, or reflectors

brightness ability of a surface to reflect or emit light; brightness of a light source is properly called *luminosity* or *luminous intensity*; brightness of a reflecting object is known as *luminance*

broad a rectangular, open-faced luminaire used for even lighting in background, bounce, and fill lighting situations

brute a large, 225-amp carbon arc fixture; the largest single fixture used in production; also refers to nine-light and 12-light PAR clusters

butterfly a large net or silk (measuring at least 4 ft × 4 ft) that is stretched on a frame and supported by a single stand; commonly used outdoors to diffuse direct sunlight

C-47 a nickname for the wooden clothespin used to clamp gels to barndoors

C-clamp a C-shaped screw clamp used to fasten a fixture to an overhead pipe or grid

C-stand *see Century stand*

camera tape a strong, 1-inch wide, cloth-backed tape; white camera tape is often used for labeling film magazines, cans, and clapper boards; black tape is used for sealing magazines and cans from light leakage; *see gaffer tape*

candela a unit of light intensity that equals the light emitted by a $1/16$-square centimeter of a black body at 2042°K (the melting point of platinum)

carbon arc a high-intensity, low-voltage lamp that creates an intense specular light by arcing electrical current between two carbon rods; is noisy and must be constantly trimmed by a technician; often used to simulate or fill in the dazzling light of the sun; the most common is the 225-amp brute

CC filters color-compensating filters; a series of filters in progressive degrees of red, green, blue, yellow, magenta, and cyan saturations; used for adjusting the color of a scene by filtering either light sources, the camera, or both; used in photographic printing

CdS cell a cadmium-sulfide, light-sensitive cell used in most reflected light meter designs; CdS cell meters require a power source, such as a battery, and measure light intensity when light falling on their surfaces creates resistance in the meter's electrical circuit; very sensitive to low light; exhibits some lag problems in changing light conditions

Century stand a three-legged, adjustable stand used to hold gobos in front of a light source

characteristic curve a graphic depiction of a film's sensitivity and contrast characteristics; consists of a curved line that represents the change of density of an image as exposure is increased

charge-coupled device (CCD) a solid-state, light-sensitive element that takes the place of a pickup tube in a video camera; registers an image on a grid of thousands of picture elements or pixels; unlike the pickup tube, is not subject to imaging defects, such as lag and comet-tailing

cheat to artificially change the position of a subject from that of another shot in the same scene to allow for a more advantageous angle or to preserve lighting continuity

cheek light a type of separation light used to give the outer contour of a subject's cheek a kick of edge light

cheek patch *see Rembrandt cheek patch*

chiaroscuro pronounced key-AR-oh-skew-roh; literally light-dark; a high-contrast modeling of light and dark values in a subject, often with very little modulation between highlight and shadow

chip *see charge-coupled device*

chip chart the nine-value scale chart used to set up video equipment

CID lamp compact iodide daylight lamp; a metal halide discharge source similar to an HMI; has a correlated color temperature of 5500°K

circuit any electrical path that includes the energy source

clothesline grip jargon; a suspended cable not properly taped to the floor or ground; a safety hazard

cluster a fixture incorporating several PAR lamp modules; used to augment or fill in sunlight

color-compensating filter *see CC filters*

color temperature the measurement of various light wavelengths, in degrees Kelvin, of the visible spectrum of a light source

conductor a material that facilitates the flow of electrical current, such as metal

contrast the relative difference between the darkest and lightest elements in an image or scene; determined not only by the relation between extremities, but by the intermediate tonal scale between light and dark; a high-contrast image exhibits very little gradation between the darkest and lightest values

contrast-viewing filter a dark glass or filter used for judging the contrast of a scene before photographing

cookie *see cukaloris*

correlated color temperature indicates a visual match when a light source is not a black body radiating source, such as a fluorescent lamp

CSI lamp compact source iodide lamp; an enclosed arc discharge lamp similar to the HMI, with a color temperature of 4400°K

CTO an amber filter for lowering color temperature of a source, usually from 5500°K to 3200°K

cukaloris an opaque sheet perforated with irregular holes; used as a gobo to create a mottled pattern on a subject or to break up the monotony of an even-colored background

cup block a wooden block, with a bowl-like depression in the top, that fits under the wheels of a rolling stand to keep it from rolling away

cut to remove light from a scene

cutter a long narrow flag

cyan one of the subtractive primaries; a mixture of blue and green

cyclorama or *cyc*; a large, smooth, curving backdrop used in studios and sound stages to create a sky or limbo effect

cyc strip a bank of open-faced fixtures placed on the ground along the bottom of a cyclorama to provide even background illumination

day-for-night a method of simulating nighttime by shooting exterior scenes during the day, when actual nighttime photography is not practical; achieved by underexposing film; using filters; shooting on sunny days, late afternoon, or early morning; and excluding the bright sky as much as possible

dichroic filter a filter that reflects certain light wavelengths while transmitting others; often used with tungsten-halogen lamps for daylight shooting

diffraction the phenomenon exhibited by wave fronts that, passing the edge of an opaque body, are modulated and result in a redistribution of energy; becomes apparent in light by the presence of closely spaced, dark and light bands at the edge of a shadow

diffusions translucent materials that soften highlights and shadows, reduce contrast, and increase the size of a source

direct current (DC) electrical current that flows continuously in one direction only; opposite of alternating current (AC)

directional light hard light that strikes in a beam of cohesive, parallel rays from one or very few angles; typically provided by a spotlight

director of photography (DP) the person responsible for capturing the image on film or video. The DP is responsible for the lighting of the set or location; the general composition of the scene; the colors of the images; the choice of cameras, lenses, and film stock; and the setting, setups, and movements of the camera. Since the DP is also responsible for maintaining an overall style and consistent balance of color and lighting, the operation of the camera itself is often handled by a second cameraperson.

discharge lamp a lamp in which light is produced by an electrical discharge in a gas-filled enclosure

dot a small, disk-shaped flag

douser a device for cutting the light beam of a fixture internally without actually extinguishing the source

dulling spray an aerosol spray applied to highly reflective surfaces to cut down glare and hot spots

duvatyne a strong, fire-retardant black fabric used for making flags and cutters; also used to black out windows, conceal objects from view, and control spill light

ear a flag set up on one side of a fixture to block spill light; also called a *sider*

eggcrate a partitioned, gridlike accessory that attaches to the front of a soft light to better direct its beam

EI *see exposure index*

electronic field production (EFP) a method of single-camera video production used extensively for producing high-quality dramatic programming; uses many motion picture production techiques, as distinguished from multicamera television and electronic news gathering

electronic news gathering (ENG) a method of shooting and videotaping news events, interviews, and other informational programming; accomplished with lightweight, portable, video equipment; similar to the 16mm documentary filmmaking that it has largely supplanted

ellipsoidal fixture an enclosed housing fixture that produces a hard, focusable beam of light; named for the shape of their reflectors; usually used as overhead fixtures on stages

emulsion the light-sensitive layer of film that contains silver halide crystals suspended in gelatin; the latent image is formed when the emulsion is exposed in the camera and made visible when the silver salts are transformed into metallic silver in developing; color film has three emulsion layers for each of the primary colors

exposure index (EI) a number designation for film sensitivity; *see ASA rating*

eye light a small barndoor or snoot spotlight mounted on or near the camera to give sparkle to the eyes and teeth of a subject

f-stop the measurement for calculating the opening of a lens aperture for determining exposure; derived by dividing the focal length of a lens by the diameter of its aperture

falloff the diminishment of illumination at progressively greater distances from its source; light falls off inversely to the square of the distance from the source to the subject

feather to move a flag or other gobo closer or farther from the source to vary the hardness of the shadow; also refers to the ragged edge on one side of a net, scrim, or silk

fill light any soft light that fills in areas of shadow cast by a key light, thereby descreasing image contrast; frequently placed near the camera on the side opposite the key

flag a rectangular frame stretched with black fabric and mounted on a C-stand and used as a gobo for shaping or blocking a beam of light

flare spill light that enters the optical system of a camera causing specular highlights and fogging

flashing the laboratory technique of exposing film to a very low level of illumination after shooting in order to reduce contrast and desaturate colors; also called *post-fogging*

flat light characterless, textureless light that casts very shallow shadows; often emanates from the direction of the camera or observer

fluorescence the property of certain substances to absorb radiation of a particular wavelength and re-emit radiation as light of a different, usually greater, wavelength; persists only as long as a stimulus remains active

fluorescent lamp a tubular lamp within which alternating current causes electrons to bombard mercury atoms that in turn stimulate the phosphors, which coat its envelope, to emit visible light; emits light primarily in five wavelengths

flux the rate of light energy measured in lumens

focus to vary a fixture's beam size and intensity

focus range the ratio of spot to flood of a lighting fixture

footcandle a measurement of light intensity based on the luminous intensity on the inside surface of a sphere with a 1-foot radius from a light source of 1 candela or standard candle; equal to 1 lumen per square foot; used widely in the United States, but most other countries use the *lux* as a measurement of light intensity

footlambert a unit of reflected light equal to the luminance of a surface that emits a luminous flux of 1 lumen per square foot; the luminance of a perfectly reflecting surface receiving 1 footcandle of illumination

front lighting general flat lighting that comes from the camera area or front of a set

gaffer the head electrician in a film or video production crew; supplies, places, operates, and maintains all lamps, fixtures, and power sources for illumination; takes instructions from the director of photography and often has several electrical assistants; *see best boy*

gaffer tape also called *grip tape*; a tough, 2-inch wide, cloth-backed tape; similar in appearance to duct tape and used for securing cables, plates, and other lighting accessories; usually gray, but available in other colors

glare light that reflects off shiny or specular surfaces

gobo any lighting accessory that is used in front or inside of a luminaire to shape or alter the quality of the beam; two commonly used gobos are the flag and the cukaloris

gray card an 8 × 10-inch card with one matte gray side and one white surface; the gray side reflects 18% of the light striking it, representing an average of all reflective values; the white side reflects approximately 90% of the light that strikes it; often used to take light readings using a reflected light meter

grid a pipe or several pipes fastened together and suspended from a ceiling above the set to support lighting fixtures

grip a stagehand responsible for many tasks on a set; may carry and set up equipment, props, and scenery; lay dolly tracks; push the dolly during shooting

hair light   a separation light that strikes the subject from behind and overhead; creates a halo effect on the head and shoulders

hard light   a relatively small, direct, and often focusable source that creates strong highlights and dense, well-defined shadows

high-key   a type of lighting that emphasizes an overall bright effect, with predominantly middle-gray to white values

hot set   a set in which more scenes must be shot

hot spot   a harsh, bright highlight within a scene

illumination   light that emanates from a source; luminous intensity; also used to describe lighting that has no craft or style

incandescence   a process by which light is produced when a substance becomes hot enough to glow

incandescent lamp   any lamp that produces light when electrical resistance causes its filament to heat up and glow; also called a *standard incandescent lamp*

incident lamp   all light that falls on a subject, as opposed to any light that reflects off the subject

incident light meter   an exposure meter that measures light that illuminates a subject, rather than light reflecting from the subject

intensity   the strength of a light source independent of the subject; luminous intensity

inverse square law   the law that states that the light intensity of a radiating source is inversely proportional to the square of the distance between the subject and the source; $LI = 1/d^2$; *see falloff*

junior   a Fresnel fixture that houses a 2000-watt lamp

Kelvin scale   a scale for measuring very high temperatures, including color temperature; is based on the Celsius scale, but begins at absolute zero ($-272\,°C$); the term *Kelvin* is often used interchangably with color temperature; *see color temperature, black body*

key light   the primary light source in a scene; represents the motivating light source

kicker   a light to the side and rear of a subject; serves as an edge and separation light

kicks   bright light reflections that add sparkle and life to a scene

kill   to extinguish a lamp

lamp   the light source in a fixture

lamp life   the amount of hours at which 50% of all test lamps fail

lavender   a light, violet-colored silk that diffuses somewhat as it cuts the light of a source; cuts light by 15%

Leko   another term for *ellipsoidal fixture*; a trade name

lexan   a tough, resilient, clear acrylic sheet material often used as a protective shield through which the camera shoots when photographing gunshots or explosions

lighting director   the person responsible for lighting video productions

lighting grid   an overhead lattice or pipelike structure to carry lighting fixtures and electrical connections

lighting ratio   the ratio of key to fill light; generally determined by comparing the fill light alone to the overlap of both key and fill lights; a high lighting ratio produces a high contrast image

limbo effect   an area of no defining characteristics; often produced by a flatly illuminated cyclorama or seamless, paper backdrop

location   an area used for shooting, or considered for use, other than a studio

low-key   a type of lighting that emphasizes a predominance of darkness and shadow, and often high contrast effects

lumen   a measure of luminous flux; 1 lumen is equal to the amount of light per second from a point source of one candlepower intensity emitted in a unit solid angle (an angle formed at the vertex of a cone)

luminous flux   the rate of flux of luminous energy; measured in lumens

lux   the international metric unit of incident light; equal to 1 lumen of luminous flux falling perpendicularly on a 1-meter square surface; 10.764 lux equals 1 footcandle

magic hour   dusk (or sometimes dawn); when exterior lighting conditions are most favorable

matte   a nonreflective, dull surface

modeling   the detailed, three-dimensional look of a subject achieved through the interplay of light and shadow

motivated lighting   lighting designed to appear to come from logical sources, as from practicals, streetlights, etc.

multicamera production   a method of television production that uses several cameras; since editing is done primarily in real time via a switcher, set lighting must be general enough to be acceptable from several camera angles simultaneously; used for talk shows, game shows, and other live programming

natural lighting   ambient lighting that emanates from sources other than lighting instruments, such as daylight, candlelight, or practical lamps

net   a C-stand-mounted gobo that cuts light intensity of a source without greatly diffusing it; usually consists of black, porous cloth; a nonelectrical dimmer

neutral density (ND) filter   a filter that cuts transmission of light without otherwise affecting its color temperature or quality; calibrated in one-third stops; an ND of .3 cuts light 1 stop

night-for-night   shooting night scenes during actual nighttime, as opposed to day-for-night or dusk-for-night

opaque   any object or material that does not transmit light in any degree

operator   the camera operator

PAR-FAY   a sealed-beam, parabolic aluminized reflector lamp that incorporates a special dichroic filter; has a color temperature that closely approximates photographic daylight and is frequently used in 2-, 4-, 6-, 9-, and 12-light clusters for outdoor fill illumination

pattern   a thin, metal cookie that can be placed in a slide and used to project a specially designed pattern of light, such as foliage or window frames, onto backdrops; often used in ellipsoidal fixtures

pepper   a small Fresnel fixture, in one of several sizes, that accomodates a 100-, 200-, 420-, 650-, or 1000-watt tungsten-halogen lamp; manufactured by LTM Corporation

plane lighting   a method of visualizing and lighting a subject or scene as a series of planes; planes are lit to different levels of brightness, often with the largest or closest objects being the darkest

polarizer   a filter that saturates colors and reduces or eliminates glare in a scene by blocking polarized light

post-fogging   *see flashing*

practical   any prop on a set that functions normally; for example, a desk lamp that serves as a light source within a scene

rag   any fabric that must be stretched on a frame for use as a net or silk

reflected light   light reflected from a surface, after losing intensity due to absorption and scattering

reflected light meter   an exposure meter that measures light reflecting from a subject, as opposed to measuring light that falls on the subject; camera through-the-lens and auto-iris metering designs use the reflected light meter system

reflector board   a large rectangular panel with one highly reflective and one soft, reflective surface; pivots in a yoke held by a heavy stand; used to fill in or augment sunlight on exterior shoots

Rembrandt cheek patch   a triangular patch of light that falls on the shadowed side of a subject's face when the key light shines at a 45° angle; a traditional starting point when setting key light position

Rembrandt lighting   a type of lighting that emphasizes light and shadow; reminiscent of certain Rembrandt paintings

rig   any assembly designed or adapted to support lights, backgrounds, and lighting accessories

rim light   a type of lighting that illuminates only the outline of a subject, often from both sides and to the rear

scrim   a wire mesh gobo used as a nonelectrical dimmer; held in the front brackets of a fixture

separation light   any light that strikes a subject from the rear, making the subject stand out from the background

set   a construction designed for the convenient lighting and shooting of scenes

set light   a term used in television production meaning background light

silhouette   dark figures and shapes that appear in contrast against a light background; generally show very little detail

silk   a diffuser that consists of a translucent silk or taffeta fabric stretched on a frame; normally mounted on a C-stand or roller stand in front of a fixture or the sun

sky pan   a fixture that consists of a bare bulb housed in a large aluminum reflector to create wide, even illumination of flat, smooth surfaces

snoot   a flanged, tube-shaped or funnel-shaped accessory that fits over the front of a fixture and focuses the light into a small circle

softlight   an open-faced fixture that features one or more indirect lamps housed in a large reflector; produces a highly diffused, nearly shadowless light

specular   a highly reflective mirrorlike surface; any bright highlights that reflect from such a surface

spill light   undesirable illumination that scatters outside the desired beam of a lamp

spot   to focus illumination of a fixture on a small area

spotlight   any luminaire capable of projecting a focused beam in a circular pattern

standard incandescent lamp   a lamp that consists of a tungsten filament set in a screwtype base with a large glass envelope filled with nitrogen gas; also called a *household bulb*; compare to tungsten-halogen lamp

strobe   an electronic light source capable of emitting light in very short bursts; useful for freezing motion; used primarily by still photographers

Streaks-n-Tips   an aerosol, hair-coloring spray sometimes used by grips and cinematographers as an applique to dim the intensity of practical lamps; used for aging props and fabrics; a trade name

striplight   a single, narrow lighting unit that contains a row of open-faced luminaires; used to illuminate cycloramas and other backgrounds

take down   to reduce the intensity of light on a subject by means of nets or scrims

talent   personnel employed as performers in a film or television production

teaser   a gobo similar to a flag

teeny   a compact, open-faced fixture with a 650-watt lamp

teeny-weeny   a compact, open-faced fixture with a 600-watt lamp

topper   a flag mounted over a light source to block top spill light

translucent   an object, material, or vapor that both transmits and scatters light in varying degrees

transparent   an object or material that transmits clear light and images without noticeable diffusion

tungsten-halogen lamp   an incandescent lamp that features a tungsten filament in a small quartz envelope filled with regenerative halogen gas; has a longer useful life than standard incandescent lamps; capable of higher wattage levels than standard incandescents

unmotivated light   light that appears to emanate from artificial or contrived sources

volt   a measure of electromotive force; equal to the potential difference that will force a current of 1 ampere through a conductor with a resistance of 1 ohm

wall spreader   a telescoping pole used as a lighting grid or light stand

waste   to gradually swivel a fixture to take down the intensity of illumination on a subject

watt   a unit of electrical power equal to the amount of work of 1 ampere under the pressure of 1 volt

wild wall   an easily removable section of a set that facilitates camera positioning and lighting

wing   to move a gobo, such as a flag, toward or away from a source in an arc

wrap   the end of a shoot when all equipment is put away and crew and cast quit for the day

BIBLIOGRAPHY

Adams, William B. *Handbook of Motion Picture Production.* New York: John Wiley and Sons, 1977.

Almendros, Nestor. *A Man with a Camera.* Trans. Rachel Phillips Belash. New York: Farrar, Straus & Giroux, 1984.

Bobker, Lee R. *Elements of Film.* 3rd ed. New York: Harcourt Brace Jovanovich, Inc., 1979.

Brouwer, Alexandra, and Thomas Lee Wright. *Working in Hollywood.* New York: Crown Publishers, Inc., 1990.

Campbell, Russel, ed. *Photographic Theory for the Motion Picture Cameraman.* New York: A.S. Barnes and Co., Inc., 1970.

———. *Photography: A Handbook of History, Materials, and Processes.* New York: A.S. Barnes and Co., Inc., 1970.

———. *Practical Motion Picture Photography.* London: The Tantivy Press, 1970.

Carlson, Verne. *Cinematographer's Survival Handbook.* Boston: Focal Press, 1987.

Carlson, Verne, and Sylvia Carlson. *Professional Cameraman's Handbook.* Boston: Focal Press, 1981.

———. *Professional Lighting Handbook.* Boston: Focal Press, 1982.

Caruso, James R., and Mavis E. Arthur. *Video Lighting and Special Effects.* New York: Prentice Hall, 1991.

Courter, Philip R. *The Filmmaker's Craft: 16mm Cinematography.* New York: Van Nostrand Reinhold Company, 1982.

Detmers, Fred, ed. *American Cinematographers Manual.* 6th ed. Hollywood: ASC Holding Corp., 1986.

Feininger, Andreas. *Light and Lighting in Photography.* New York: Amphoto, 1976.

Hunter, Fil, and Paul Fuqua. *Light—Science and Magic: An Introduction to Photographic Lighting.* Boston: Focal Press, 1990.

Madsen, Roy Paul. *Working Cinema: Learning from the Masters.* Belmont, CA: Wadsworth Publishing Co., 1990.

Malkiewicz, J. Kris. *Cinematography: A Guide for Film Makers and Film Teachers.* 2nd ed. New York: Van Nostrand Reinhold Company, 1989.

———. *Film Lighting.* New York: Prentice Hall Press, 1986.

Mathias, Harry, and Richard Patterson. *Electronic Cinematography: Achieving Photographic Control over the Video Image.* Belmont, CA: Wadsworth Publishing Co., 1985.

Mercer, John. *An Introduction to Cinematography.* Champaign, IL: Stipes Publishing Co., 1971.

Millerson, Gerald. *The Technique of Lighting for Television and Motion Pictures.* London: Focal Press, 1982.

Patterson, Richard, and Dana White, eds. *Electronic Production Techniques.* Hollywood: ASC Holding Corp., 1985.

Ritsko, Alan J. *Lighting for Location Motion Pictures.* New York: Van Nostrand Reinhold, 1979.

Samuelson, David W. *Motion Picture Camera and Lighting Equipment: Choice and Technique.* 2nd ed. Boston: Focal Press, 1986.

———. *Motion Picture Camera Techniques.* 2nd ed. Boston: Focal Press, 1984.

Schaefer, Dennis, and Larry Salvato. *Masters of Light: Conversations with Contemporary Cinematographers.* Berkeley: University of California Press, 1984.

Souto, H. Mario Raimondo. *The Technique of the Motion Picture Camera.* 4th ed. Boston: Focal Press, 1982.

Weigand, Ingrid. *Professional Video Production.* White Plains, NY: Knowledge Industry Publications, 1985.

Wilson, Anton. *Anton Wilson's Cinema Workshop.* Hollywood: ASC Holding Corp., 1983.

Young, Freddie, and Paul Petzold. *The Work of the Motion Picture Cameraman.* New York: Hastings House Publishers, 1972.